Glorious Is Thy Name!
B. B. McKinney: The Man and His Music

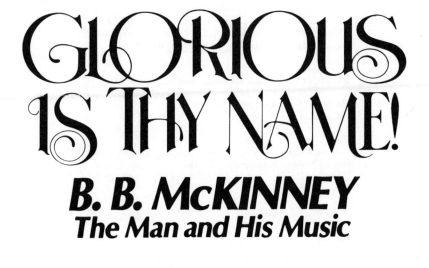

GLORIOUS IS THY NAME!

B. B. McKINNEY
The Man and His Music

Robert J. Hastings

BROADMAN PRESS
Nashville, Tennessee

Dewey Decimal Classification: B
Subject Heading: MCKINNEY, BENJAMIN BAYLESS
Library of Congress Catalog Card Number: 85-26948
Printed in the United States of America

Library of Congress Cataloging-in-Publication Data

Hastings, Robert J.
 Glorious is Thy name!

 Bibliography: p. 158
 1. McKinney, B. B., b. 1886. 2. Gospel musicians—
United States—Biography. I. Title.
ML410.M453H4 1986   783.7′092′4 [B]   85-26948
ISBN 0-8054-7230-4

DEDICATED TO
THAT ANONYMOUS STUDENT AT
SOUTHWESTERN BAPTIST THEOLOGICAL SEMINARY
WHO, FOUR DAYS BEFORE CHRISTMAS OF 1923,
WROTE TO B. B. MCKINNEY:

Inasmuch as I have not the tact to tell you, I am adopting this plan of saying how much I appreciate your song, "Carry Your Burden With a Smile."

Sometimes when I come to school, having had scarcely anything for breakfast, feeling the sidewalk dampness through the thin soles of my wornout shoes, the holes in the toes of my socks doing their utmost to climb out of my shoe tops, we sing, "Carry Your Burden With a Smile."

The spirit of the song may not change my face much, but sure charges my spiritual batteries. It puts the soft pedal on the wolf which often howls at our door. . . .

Sincerely,
A Student

"Let me write the songs of a nation, and I care not who makes its laws"—Daniel O'Connell.

"B. B. McKinney became an *institution* by himself, not only of Southern Baptists, but wherever his wonderful songs are sung . . . . While we love his songs, we love him best because of his simple, rugged, manly Christian character"—E. Leslie Carlson.

This anthem-like hymn, written late in his career, typi-
fies McKinney's lifelong quest to glorify Christ:

Glorious Is Thy Name

1. Bless - ed Sav - ior, we a - dore thee, We thy love and grace pro-claim;
2. Great Re-deem - er, Lord and Mas-ter, Light of all e - ter - nal days;
3. From the throne of heav-en's glo - ry To the cross of sin and shame,
4. Come, O come, im - mor - tal Sav - ior, Come and take thy roy - al throne;

Thou art might-y, thou art ho - ly, Glo-rious is thy match-less name!
Let the saints of ev - 'ry na - tion Sing thy just and end-less praise!
Thou didst come to die a ran-som, Guilt-y sin - ners to re-claim!
Come, and reign, and reign for - ev - er, Be the king-dom all thine own!

Glo - ri-ous, Glo - ri-ous,

Glo-rious is thy name, O Lord! Glo-rious is thy name, O Lord!

Glo-rious is thy name, O Lord! Glo - ri - ous,

Glo-rious is thy name, O Lord!

Glo - ri-ous, Glo-rious is thy name, O Lord! A - MEN.

Glo-rious is thy name, O Lord!

Preface

It was August of 1946, a year after the end of World War II. The place was Falls Creek Baptist Assembly in the Arbuckle Mountains near Davis, Oklahoma.

I was one of 9,150 who gathered there in August for ten days of music, preaching, inspiration, and recreation. Excitement ran high as the assembly reopened after wartime shortages of food, gasoline, and tires had closed it during the summers of 1943, 1944, and 1945.

It was all so new and strange to me, a first-year student from Southwestern Baptist Seminary in Fort Worth. Coming from Illinois, where our tiny Baptist encampment was like a postage stamp in comparison, I was impressed with the thousands of young people who overflowed the big tabernacle twice daily, many spilling out on the grassy slopes on quilts, lawn chairs, and camp stools.

Too, I was impressed with B. B. McKinney, the legendary gospel songwriter who had directed the singing every summer since 1925. And by E. E. "Hot Dog" Lee, the effervescent B.Y.P.U. "field worker" for the Baptist Sunday School Board who had taught at every session but one since 1917. And by English evangelist Charlie Taylor, the energetic assembly preacher who captivated us with his clipped British accent, contagious humor, and prizefighter-like antics.

But the greatest of these, to me, was B. B. McKinney.

I suppose I was aware of McKinney, for I'd grown up on *The Modern Hymnal* and *The Broadman Hymnal* in the First Baptist Church in Marion, Illinois, singing his favorite compositions such as "Satisfied with Jesus," "Have Faith in God," and "'Neath the Old Olive Trees."

But actually seeing this 6'3" giant of warmth and friendliness as he led us to mountain peaks of congregational singing was something else.

Especially inspiring was "Glorious Is Thy Name," which he'd written just four years earlier.

The congregation always laughed when he repeated what came to be his trademark: "Now if there's anyone here who can't sing or won't sing, let's send him to Sing Sing (Prison) until he does sing!"

Then a hush fell on everyone as he added, "During the recent war when my two sons were in such danger, friends questioned how I could keep singing. I told them I sang before Gene and B. B., Jr. were born, and that although I was naturally concerned for their safety, I was still singing. And if in God's grace they returned safely, I'd keep on singing. But if they never came back, my singing heart would continue to praise my Lord."

Little did we realize that this popular gospel songwriter, now in his sixtieth year, was only six years from his rendezvous with death on a rain-slick highway near Cherokee, North Carolina.

Then in early 1952, I spent five days with McKinney when he came for a music week at the University Baptist Church in Carbondale, Illinois, where I was pastor. Each evening he led a singspiration, taught a book, *Practical Music Lessons,* and rehearsed our choir for a closing concert.

But strangely, I have no memory of that week in Carbondale. I think I know why. McKinney made such a positive and even overwhelming first impression on me in Oklahoma that somehow I never got over it.

Still later I met Mrs. McKinney. It was the fall of 1955 when I moved to Nashville as a staff member of the Southern Baptist Executive Committee. Our offices were then housed in the Baptist Sunday School Board. I remember Mrs. McKinney, his widow of three years, as she worked part-time keeping study course records. She often came to our floor to say hello to her nephew, Porter W. Routh. Soft-spoken and quiet, she greeted me with a smile and a good word when I met her in the hallway or on the elevator.

As the centennial of McKinney's birth approached, Broadman Press and the Church Music Department of the Baptist Sunday School Board invited me to write an "authorized" biography, to be published in 1986.

My assignment was to write a person-centered biography, one that would capture his warmth and spirit.

Broadman Press editors had liked my oral history of the Illinois Baptist State Association, published during the Bicentennial in 1976. That book, *We Were There,* was based on interviews with a cross-section of Illinoisans. Their stories were published in the first person, with emphasis on people rather than dates and statistics.

Could I duplicate this with a biography of McKinney? Well, yes and no. McKinney had been dead for over thirty years. His widow was ninety-three, her memory failing. John, the last of his brothers and sisters, had died in 1976.

On the other hand, there were McKinney collections of photographs, clippings, and correspondence in the Dargan Research Library in Nashville and the library of Oklahoma Baptist University in Shawnee, Oklahoma. And there were nieces and nephews and friends and fellow workers who remembered him.

So in 1983, I set out on a search for the "real" B. B. McKinney. By that I mean a verbal photograph, a word picture. My goal was not a "nuts and bolts" biography that dots every *i* and crosses every *t*. Rather, I was on a search for impressions.

I ran into a few discrepancies. One enthusiastic person told how in 1944 he heard McKinney introduce one of his songs "for the first time, whereupon it spread like wildfire over the country." The truth is that hymn had already been published in 1940 in *The Broadman Hymnal!*

But that doesn't matter. What counts is that years later, someone *remembers* how a certain hymn first impressed him, first touched his life.

Earlier works have gone into details. I have sought the man.

But where could I tap that vast reservoir of memories treasured by thousands who had sat in his classes at Southwestern Seminary or rubbed shoulders with him in hundreds of revivals, conventions, and summer assemblies throughout the South and Southwest?

I devised a plan that surprised me with its success. I wrote a form "letter to the editor" to several Baptist state papers. In this, I solicited letters from readers who had known McKinney. This unleashed a flood of letters—some neatly typed on crisp stationery, others scribbled by aging hands on ordinary tablet paper.

But the message was the same, over and over—"I was saved when he led the singing in our church revival. . . . I sat at his table one day at Ridgecrest. . . . One of his songs touched me to give my life in Christian service."

More than anything, these letters convinced me that B. B. McKinney's contribution was his person as much as his songs. Hopefully, this book will make him come alive to those who never knew him.

So in truth, the research for this biography was not in libraries alone, but with folks who knew him. They are the real authors! I merely listened and recorded what they said. And if someone had not taken time to do so, many of these precious memories would in a few years be lost to posterity.

The high point of my research was in August of 1983 when Mrs. Hastings and I drove to San Antonio, Texas. There I spent two long mornings in conversations with Mrs. McKinney. In the afternoons I talked with their sons, Baylus, Jr., and Eugene, where I learned the significance of their Dad's comments about them at Falls Creek in 1946. Serving under Gen. George Patton, Eugene won a battlefield commission in Europe in 1945. And Baylus, Jr., during World War II, ferried bombers over the North and South Atlantic for a year. Later he flew hospital planes evacuating the wounded from Europe, plus other missions to the Middle East and the Far East. In all, he made over two hundred Atlantic crossings.

One of my many correspondents was Verby Lee Balinas of Houston, Texas. She described how she met B. B. McKinney about 1933 at Dry Creek Baptist Encampment in Louisiana. "I think the people came from deep in the woods every evening to attend services in a big tabernacle with sawdust on the ground. That was fifty years ago. . . ." She ended by saying, "Thanks for opening the gates of my mind to such pleasant memories."

If this book opens a memory treasure in your mind—or if it introduces you for the first time to B. B. McKinney as a person—then I have succeeded. Now, let's start by visiting in imagination that five-room, split-log house near Heflin, Louisiana, where he was born in 1886. . . .

Robert J. Hastings
Springfield, Illinois

Contents

1.
"I Just Wrote from My Heart"   15

2.
"I Like the Way You Sing"   31

3.
"Sometimes I'd Hold His Hand"   51

4.
"We Were Feeling Our Way"   67

5.
"He Lifted Me Over the Gate"   99

6.
"We Always Sing in a Major Key"   111

7.
"I Am Just Going Over Home"   123

8.
"She's Mine, If I Can Get Her!"   137

9.
"Singing Is for Believers"   151

For Further Reading   158

McKinney's revision of this New Orleans jazz classic illustrates his Louisiana roots. Popularized in New Orleans funerals in the 1890s, it may have originated in the Bahamas:

When the Saints Go Marching In.

Words adapted and
Written by B. B McK.

Arr by B. B. McKinney

1. I had a lov-ing broth-er, Death re-leased him from sin,
2. I had a pre-cious sis-ter, She has gone on be-fore,
3. I have a Christ-like fa-ther, Far be-yond the blue skies,
4. I have a dear, sweet moth-er, Sing-ing 'round the white throne,
5. I have a liv-ing Sav-ior, He re-deemed me from sin;

And I prom-ised I would meet him, When the saints go march-ing in.
And I prom-ised I would meet her On that hap-py, gold-en shore.
And some day I'll sure-ly meet him, Where there'll be no sad good-byes.
And I prom-ised I would meet her; "There we'll know as we are known."
Oh, how sweet 'twill be to meet Him, When the saints go march-ing in.

CHORUS.

When the saints . . . . . go march-ing in, ...
Oh, when the saints go march-ing in,

When the saints go march-ing in; . . . . Lord, I want to
go march-ing in;

be in that num-ber, ... When the saints go marching in.
in that num-ber,

1
"I Just Wrote from My Heart"

About 1875, a twenty-two-year-old Irishman with the impressive name of James Alexander Calvin McKinney migrated to Louisiana from Oglethorp, Georgia. James' father, Alexander F. McKinney, had in turn emigrated to the United States from Antrim County, Ireland.

After arriving in the States, Alexander had graduated from Edgefield Seminary (now Furman University). For a while, he was principal of Oglethorpe Seminary.

Neither Alexander nor James knew that someday they would be the grandfather and father of Southern Baptists' best-loved gospel songwriter, Baylus Benjamin McKinney.

Calvin* homesteaded 180 acres near Heflin in the northwest corner of Louisiana, not far from Shreveport. On this farm, he built a five-room house made of split logs. The flat sides of the logs formed the inside walls. The rounded sides were the exterior. The logs were peeled but unpainted. The floors were bare, white pine.

He built stick fireplaces at either end of the house, plus two full-length porches which ran down both sides of the house.

Calvin also erected a big, double-pin barn and grew cotton, peanuts, corn, and sugar cane, plus all sorts of vegetables. In 1876 he married Martha (Mattie) Annis Heflin and they lived in this house until 1911, when they moved to Pineville. Here, during the space of twenty-three years, Mattie gave birth to eight boys and three girls. The fourth of those boys was B. B. McKinney, born on Thursday, July 22, 1886.

---

*James McKinney went by Calvin or "Cal." From here on, he will be referred to as Calvin. His wife, Martha, went by "Mattie," the name used throughout this book.

The Heflin ancestors of Mattie, who were Scotch, had come to Louisiana from Alabama.

Although B. B. McKinney grew to be a 6'3" giant of a man weighing at least 220 pounds, his father, Calvin, was shorter than his wife, Mattie.

In a family portrait made about 1899, Calvin appears as a bushy-haired, short but muscular man, with squinty eyes and a handlebar mustache which turned down. Mattie's straight hair is pulled back tightly in a bun, her eyes round and trusting.

"All the McKinneys were strong," Winborn Davis told me. Winborn, a son of Joanna, one of the three McKinney daughters, said Calvin could carry a 360-pound barrel of flour, with no handles, for a hundred feet. He often bet that he could roll that same barrel up his legs and knees, then balance it on his shoulders. "And I have a daughter, Joanna, who can do the same thing!" he boasted. His wife, Mattie, a devout woman, frowned on these betting episodes.

Winborn knew from experience that his mother, Joanna, was strong like her father: "When I got into a scuffle with one of my brothers, she could pick up both of us by our galluses at the same time while she carried us inside to give us a spanking."

In addition to farming, Calvin was a timber estimator for various lumber companies. At one time he managed a sawmill.

Calvin also had a lifelong interest in music, which undoubtedly influenced B. B. And this same interest must have rubbed off on all the children, for they were widely known as a singing family.

Calvin attended singing or "normal" schools taught by such well-known musicians as Aldine Kieffer and E. T. Hildebrand. Both of these men taught "seven-shape" notation—that is, how to read music by the shape of the notes. This method, using diamond, square, triangle, and half-circle shaped notes, enabled students to sing and play instruments without learning the keys, the names of the notes, or lines and spaces.

Calvin admired these teachers so much that he named two of his eight sons for them—Washington Aldine Kieffer and John Hildebrand. And Calvin himself later taught singing schools in and around Heflin.

Calvin also taught basic music theory to his own son, B. B., as well as the other children, using one of Hildebrand's textbooks, *First Lessons in Sing-*

ing. Calvin McKinney developed a strong admiration for a third music teacher, Charles J. Gilbert, whom he met one summer at a "normal" school. Gilbert, an evangelistic singer, composer, and music publisher, exerted a strong influence on Baptist music throughout Louisiana.

In years to come, Calvin McKinney would on three occasions send his son, B. B., to schools where Gilbert taught. He early sensed the musical talent in B. B. and until his death dreamed of the day when B. B. would give himself to a musical career.

B. B.'s very first "formal" training in music was at a singing school at near Fryeburg, then called Hope. It was taught by J. D. Smith.

Although Calvin wasn't a professing Christian until 1912 (two years before his death), he did lead the singing at the Bistineau Baptist Church. This is the church four miles from the McKinney home, which the family attended. Preaching services were held once a month. But when one of the members commented that he felt it was wrong for non-Christians to hold offices in the church, Calvin grew upset and quit.

Much has been written about the reed organ which Calvin bought from a mail-order house in about 1900. It came by train, and the boys hauled it home by wagon from the station in Heflin. The twenty-mile-or-so round-trip took them all day.

This organ became the focal point for family singings—not just on Sundays, but also at nights during the week, after the farm work was done.

A number of authors have written that once the organ arrived and the McKinney family realized no one could play it, they chose Carrie, one of the daughters, to learn. This sounds good in print until one realizes that in 1900, Carrie was only two years old! It's true, however, that Carrie later took music lessons and often accompanied the family singings.

Carrie remembered as a little girl sitting on the porch after supper, listening to B. B. play his harmonica. He told her how his Dad had taught him his first notes as they worked in the fields. He also told how he had composed words for the older hymn tunes, then tore them up without showing them to anyone.

Years later, when fellow workers were going through his desk at the Baptist Sunday School Board in Nashville following his death, they found this note on yellow paper in his handwriting:

> I began composing little tunes to old hymn words when I was
> only eight. I composed these tunes as I plowed in the fields. I
> knew nothing of how to write them down. I just wrote them from
> my mind and heart.

So apparently he began by writing words to existing tunes, as well as
tunes to existing words.

It was around the organ the children learned to harmonize, B. B. singing
baritone, while Will sang bass, Tom, high tenor, Kieffer, second tenor, and
John, almost any part.

More than once, Mattie, their mother, would interrupt, "Do you really
mean what you're singing?" T. L. Holcomb recalled how years later, B. B.
was leading the singing in a Baptist meeting in Denton, Texas. All of a sud-
den, while they were singing "Sweet Hour of Prayer," B. B. stopped and
asked: "Is it a sweet hour? If it ever becomes a burden in your life to pray,
you had better pray longer, and stay with God more securely, because
something is pulling you away."

Others remember similar instances when B. B. rephrased his mother's
question in public services, "Do you really mean the words you're singing?"

B. B.'s mother, Mattie, was known as a woman of prayer and piety. According to Paul R. Powell, one of McKinney's biographers, people from
miles around visited their home on horseback or wagon for her prayers and
advice.

"Pick" Coleman was the name of a black man who lived nearby and often worked for the McKinneys for wages. At least 6'3" himself, Coleman
could make a good twelve-foot swath as he swung an oak cradle with a
four-foot blade. He once told Winborn Davis, "The McKinney boys were
good workers, but I could work any of them down."

One afternoon Pick was standing by the well-shed apart from the other
workers waiting for the supper call. Mattie McKinney slipped out of the
house to talk with Pick, who wasn't a Christian. A revival was in progress
at the Mount Nebo Baptist Church where Pick attended.

"Pick, I've been praying for you," she said softly. Pick looked at the
ground. "Thank you, Miss Mat, I've been a-prayin' about it myself."

She asked if he'd kneel with her there in the yard for prayer, which he did. That night he made a profession of faith at Mount Nebo Church.

In 1917, when Mattie McKinney's body was brought home from Pineville for burial, Pick stood beside B. B. in the parlor before her coffin. He wiped his eyes on a soiled shirt sleeve and said, "She led me to Jesus, Mr. Ben."

Throughout his life, B. B. McKinney was known for his unending sense of humor. Winborn E. Davis, one of his nephews, says he could see the funny side of anything. Someone might fall in a mud puddle, but B. B. couldn't help laughing while pulling him out. With the best of humor he might say, "You looked like a cow falling into a dipping vat."

"His humor wasn't hostile or aggressive; nor did he embarrass with a horse laugh," Winborn added. "He chuckled in a soft, easy way."

"He was a good worker, but mischievous. When picking cotton, he would fall behind on purpose, then bounce a green cotton boll off one of his brothers' backs. By the time they looked around, B. B. was picking cotton like mad, whistling and looking as innocent as a baby.

"Other times while hoeing cotton or corn, he'd get behind one of his brothers or a hired hand, slide the end of his hoe handle on the ground between their feet, and yell 'Snake!' He had a ready supply of practical jokes that kept things lively on the farm."

If the McKinney children fell to quarreling, their mother sang softly:

> Let us gather up sunbeams,
> Lying all around our path,
> Let us keep the wheat and roses,
> Casting out the thorns and chaff.
>
> Then scatter seeds of kindness,
> Then scatter seeds of kindness,
> Then scatter seeds of kindness,
> For our reaping by and by.

One of B. B.'s pranks almost backfired. He and Tom, just older than he, liked to hunt. One day while hunting quail they crossed their Grandpa Heflin's cow pasture which adjoined the McKinney farm. Their Dad had just bought a Belgian hexagonal barrel, single shot, .32 caliber rifle. It had a peculiar upright hammer that could be half or full cocked.

Ben, with the rifle on half cock, spotted his Grandpa's prize bull about a hundred yards away. Thinking the rifle wouldn't fire on half cock, Ben boasted, "I'll bet I can hit him right between the eyes."

"Bet you can't," Tom dared.

With that, B. B. pulled the trigger. To his surprise, the gun not only fired but the bull collapsed on the ground. Frozen with fear, the brothers walked over to the bull, which had a small lump and a spot of blood on his forehead. When B. B. nudged the bull with his foot to see if he were really dead, he jumped up, snorted, and ran away. B. B. and Tom realized the only thing that saved them was the minimum load cartridge and their distance. They said nothing to Grandpa Heflin and if he ever noticed anything unusual, he never mentioned it.

Bigger than other children his age, B. B. seemed to have an apparent lack of fear or feeling of embarrassment. Friends couldn't always tell whether his behavior was intentionally funny or just spontaneous. If something turned up embarrassing, it didn't seem to bother him.

An example was his first day in Hope School at nearby Fryeburg. Each child brought his lunch in a syrup bucket or similar container. After just an hour or so of school, B. B. casually got up from his seat, picked up his lunch pail, and headed for the door. When the teacher asked where he was going, he replied, "Oh, I was going to eat me a sweet 'tater." The entire classroom echoed with laughter while the teacher explained the rules. He shrugged his shoulders, grinned, sat down and said, "I thought people were supposed to eat when they're hungry."

How was life on a red clay, Louisiana farm in the late 1800s in a five-room house with a family of eleven children? No immediate member of the family is living to tell us. But again, Winborn E. Davis comes up with vivid descriptions.

Winborn, a nephew of B. B., lived in the McKinney house from 1917 to about 1924. By then B. B. was a grown man, living in Fort Worth, Texas. But the style of living had not changed all that much. Winborn says the way he lived there as a boy is the way B. B. lived.

Winborn's parents moved to the McKinney place in 1917 to raise two of the younger children, after both Calvin and Mattie McKinney had died. Winborn's mother was Joanna, one of B. B.'s sisters. Since Joanna had eight children of her own, this made a total of ten children plus the two adults, or twelve in all.

"Since there were only five rooms, we slept in every room except the kitchen," Winborn said. "As kids, we slept crosswise in trundle beds. Mother cooked on a wood-fired range which had a big reservoir for heating water. I remember the bare floor of wide pine—no carpeting. We scrubbed the floors with cornshuck brooms and homemade lye soap. From a nearby spring, we hauled in white sand which we sprinkled on the floors once they were cleaned.

"Each spring we rolled crabgrass and red-clay mud into what we called 'mud caps,' about fourteen inches long. We patted them onto protruding nails, both inside and outside the two chimneys. During the winter, the mud would have caked and fallen off, creating a fire hazard.

"We raised cotton for our cash crop. We ate all our corn, going to the gristmill at Heflin every Saturday where it was ground into meal on the shares. The millers kept one of every five buckets. In the fall we stored potatoes in a dirt bank covered with straw. We also raised sugarcane, which we took to a neighbor who owned a sugarmill. Our share was 120 gallons of the syrup, for we easily used over two gallons a week.

"We also planted several acres of crowder peas, peanuts, oats for animals, plus a big garden of snap and butter beans, potatoes, peas, carrots, cabbage, turnips, mustard, tomatoes, and lots of popcorn (for popcorn balls on Sunday afternoons). Mother served five to eight of those vegetables at a typical meal. We also raised berries as well as a small orchard of peaches, apples, and plums. On white cloths Mother dried fruit, which she spread on top of the sheds and later made into cobblers and fried pies.

"A typical breakfast included ninety-two large biscuits. Mother made that exact number religiously, scooping flour from a big barrel. She also put two pounds of butter on the table, two dozen fried eggs, sliced ham, bacon, or stuffed sausage, plus cane syrup.

"In a half-gallon syrup bucket, she packed my school lunches of a boiled egg, sliced fried sweet potato, fruit pies, and cold biscuits with a hole punched in the top filled with syrup."

So the years passed for B. B. McKinney on the quiet Louisiana farm— 1890, 1892, 1894, 1896, 1898, and finally 1900, the start of the twentieth century—untouched by radio, television, or daily newspapers. Saturday trips to the mill at Heflin, a new baby brother or sister every two or three years, snatches of education at the Hope School two miles south of their home, services at the Bistineau Baptist Church four miles away (sometimes taking short cuts across the fields and woods, their mother breaking a path through the underbrush).

And always the singing . . . around the family organ, on the porch with the harmonica, B. B. serving as "lead" worker in the fields, singing in rhythm with the workers as they chopped cotton. Most impressive of all—at least to B. B.—was his mother singing about the house:

> I am a poor wayfaring stranger,
> While traveling thro' this world below;
> There is no sickness, toil, nor danger
> In that bright world to which I go.
>
> I'm going there to meet my father,
> I'm going there no more to roam;
> I am just going over Jordan,
> I am just going over home.

In later years he would sing it as a solo himself, hundreds of times, in dozens of states, until he sang it for the last time ten days before his death in 1952.

Another outlet for B. B.'s musical talents, according to his sister Carrie, was singing at "closing school exercises." While the "stage" at Hope School was being rearranged between acts, he entertained with songs, such as "The Wine Cup Did It All," which he once sang following a pantomime on the evils of crime.

In 1902, at the age of sixteen, B. B. decided to drop out of the little one-room log school at Fryeburg to work in a sawmill, where his Dad was the foreman. He also found jobs in a cotton mill and in the lumber camps, where the "rough-necks" or fellow workers nicknamed him old "Hi-Pocket." But still he kept singing and composing simple tunes, while his Dad continued his dream for more musical training for his children.

Then came a day in 1906, a pivotal year in B. B.'s life. While sawing with a fellow named Cobb, B. B. told him that "tomorrow will be my last day in the woods," that he was "going to school at Mount Lebanon."

So shortly after Christmas he enrolled at Mount Lebanon Baptist Academy near Arcadia, about thirty miles from the McKinney home. His Dad was pleased to see him go, for his old friend, C. G. Gilbert, was on the faculty. Here B. B. would get his first formal training in music.

The late B. B. Cox, once an evangelist with the Home Mission Board, remembered standing with a group of fellow students on the campus the Sunday afternoon McKinney arrived. "Boys, I'm B. B. McKinney," he began. "I'm a log cutter and I've come up here to get a little education. But I'm dead broke. Do you fellows know where I can get in a crap game and earn a little money for tuition and food?" Dressed in overalls and a blue shirt, he was carrying a small bag. Cox explained that Mount Lebanon was a Baptist school that didn't allow gambling, not even games of any kind on Sundays. B. B. expressed surprise, saying he didn't know that shooting craps was a sin, but that he'd never engage in it again.

However, he continued with his little pranks and practical jokes and before long was expelled and sent home in the middle of the week. "What are you doing home this time of the week?" his Dad inquired. "I'm home to stay," B. B. said, explaining why he got expelled.

"Well, you're not staying here," his Dad warned. "I sent you to Mount Lebanon to learn and I expect you to do just that. You turn right around and march back and apologize and finish your studies."

B. B. knew better than to argue with his 165-pound wiry father, the Irishman, so he obeyed. Back on campus, the principal showed surprise when Ben said, "Dad sent me back and I promise not to cause any more trouble."

The principal protested, "But you can't stay. I sent you home to stay and I mean it."

With that, B. B. pulled himself up to his 6'3" frame, looked down at the smallish principal, and said, "Apparently you didn't hear what I said. I said I'm back in school to stay and behave myself." And stay he did.

Although reared in a Christian home, B. B. was twenty-three years old before he accepted Christ as Savior. It was during his third term at Mount Lebanon. His conversion was not a dramatic one. One night, unable to sleep and deeply disturbed over his spiritual condition, he sat up and prayed until assurance came.

When I read about his conversion, I thought of what his mother, Mattie, had written in the family Bible. In her careful but quaint penmanship is listed the birthdate of each of her eleven children, even including the day of the week, such as "on Saturday, Oct. 22nd, 1881."

Then at the bottom she added, "And may God bless and save them is the prayer of the Mother." For B. B., her prayer was now answered. That same fall he began leading the singing in revivals and continued to do so until he left Louisiana six years later for Fort Worth, Texas to enter Southwestern Baptist Seminary.

During those six years, he taught singing schools and helped in as many as two hundred revivals in Louisiana churches, often with an evangelist by the name of Allen Pinckney Durham. A. P. Durham (nicknamed "Apple Pie"), pastor of about forty quarter-time Louisiana churches as well as evangelist for the state convention, encouraged McKinney in every way. "Uncle Pinck started me out as a gospel singer," B. B. noted later.

Today, when high school and college are taken for granted, it's not easy to imagine the giant step B. B. took when he left the farm and the sawmills in 1906. Inman Johnson, a professor at Southern Baptist Seminary in Louisville, Kentucky and longtime friend, remembers B. B. telling him he didn't own a pair of shoes until "I left the sawmill country of Louisiana" for school. He apparently meant dress shoes, for surely the McKinney children didn't go barefoot in winter. Or did they?

And Artie S. Vernado of Jackson, Louisiana, a one-time neighbor of the McKinneys when they lived in Pineville, Louisiana, remembers B. B. telling her how as a young man he so badly wanted a suit, which his family couldn't afford. His mother took fertilizer sacks, dyed them a beautiful brown with dye made from the bark of a red oak tree, and handmade his first suit.

In his own words, B. B. recalls one of those early revivals in rural churches: "A farmer invited me home with him for dinner. After we'd eaten, I sat at their old reed organ and played and sang for the family, doing my best to make a favorable impression on his beautiful daughter. After I'd finished my concert, I asked my farmer host if he thought I should 'cultivate' my voice. He told me not to bother, just to plow it all under!"

Sallie Harkness Johnson, R.N., who last worked at the Baptist Children's Home in Monroe, Louisiana, recalls when B. B. would lead summer revivals back home in the Bistineau Baptist Church. Sallie wrote me on Sept. 22, 1983 from Minden, Louisiana, when she was eighty-one:

> In those days we had what we called protracted meetings under brush arbors, with coal oil lanterns hung on poles. My mother always sang in the choir, while Pa-Pa (that was what we called our father) took care of the children. And did we know to be still and quiet!
>
> At the beginning of the meeting, Pa-Pa would ask B. B. to set a day for the entire choir to take dinner at our house. Once a day had been set, the hired hands helped butcher a pig and a goat which we barbecued the night before (no refrigeration). Mama would cook for two days, while the black help on our place got the news around that Mr. B. B. McKinney was coming to Mr. Harkness' house for dinner!
>
> Members of the choir would come in a wagon and Mama spread tables under the trees for everyone to eat. What a day never to be forgotten! After dinner, Pa-Pa moved the piano out on the porch and what a singing big time we had with Carrie McKinney at the piano. The yard would be filled with black people. Now almost all have passed away, but I enjoy these memories. This was every summer, not just one year. How we looked forward to it. Just yesterday I spent the afternoon with one of B. B.'s nieces in Heflin.

Now back to B. B.'s schooling. Sometime between 1906 and 1910 he and his brother Tom and sister Alitha moved to Winnfield for a year of high school. Why? You've probably guessed the answer. C. J. Gilbert was on the faculty that year, and Calvin McKinney never missed a chance for his children to study music under him.

The three McKinney siblings set up housekeeping "in the old Fitch house in the 1100 block of Center Street." While the date is uncertain, records show that B. B. played tackle on the 1909 Winnfield high school football team, and brother Tom played right guard. It was the first year for football at Winnfield. Mickey O'Quin, who later practiced law in Shreveport, reportedly brought the first football to town.

It is said that Huey P. "Kingfish" Long (1893-1935), later a colorful governor of Louisiana and U.S. senator, attended the same high school.

In the fall of 1910, Calvin McKinney saw to it that his aspiring musical son, B. B., enrolled at Louisiana College in Pineville, where he studied until May of 1913. He played football there too, at least on the 1910-11 team. He also led singing at the new First Baptist Church in Pineville, where he was a charter member along with C. J. Gilbert and A. P. Durham.

By 1911 Calvin and Mattie McKinney decided to rent out the family farm near Heflin and move to Pineville so all the children could go to college easily. Yes, C. J. Gilbert was now on the faculty at Louisiana College, and head of the music department! Among other subjects, B. B. studied harmony, voice, and sight reading. He later said, "Charles Gilbert meant more to me in a musical way than any other musician. The fundamentals he taught me have stayed with me through the years."

In a letter written in 1984, Artie S. Varnado of Jackson, Louisiana shared her memories of living next to the McKinneys in Pineville:

> I am now 76 and I was eight years old when my parents moved to Pineville so we could be near Louisiana College. One of my fondest childhood memories is when the McKinneys moved in across the street and brought their family organ. There were six of us children in the Sylvest family (my maiden name) and it was with delight that we were always invited to prayer meetings and singings at the McKinneys'.
>
> The McKinney boys were grown young men and it was always a delight when they came home and sang together. I was impressed with their harmonizing voices.
>
> Grandma (Mattie) McKinney was a delightful Christian, active in the W.M.U. Once when my mother had a new baby, Mrs. McKinney brought a nice tray of food. Mam couldn't eat all of it so she offered some to my little brother. We older kids thought it was real funny when he said, "Mama, will I catch what you have if I eat after you?"

There was lots of sickness during those years and I remember how Mrs. McKinney sat up with us many nights. One of my greatest griefs was when Mrs. McKinney took sick and died. It wasn't long until the McKinney family moved (back to the farm near Heflin). Before they left, they gave Mrs. McKinney's sewing chair to Mama. It was homemade, with a cowhide seat. Years later I talked with B. B. McKinney when he was speaking at Baton Rouge. He remembered his mother sitting many hours in that chair, sewing for her family, while she sang to herself, "No, Never Alone."

Sister Carrie remembered that both Tom and B. B. sang in "the famous Louisiana College male quartet" and that they were "widely known and traveled over most of the South."

But for some reason, B. B. dropped out of Louisiana College in May of 1913 and took a job as clerk at Barnett's Store in Pineville, which sold general dry goods. He also attended a business school in Alexandria briefly. Tom dropped out to get married. All of this disappointed their father, Calvin, who still dreamed of musical careers for some of his children.

Calvin McKinney died suddenly one night in February of 1914, a year before B. B. entered Southwestern Baptist Seminary in Fort Worth, Texas. He never lived to see his illustrious son make a definite commitment for a church-centered music career.

However, in 1912, two years before his death, Calvin made a profession of faith in Christ, something his wife, Mattie, had prayed for since 1876.

I am indebted to Jerome P. Owens of Woodville, Texas for an account of his conversion. Owens heard the story when he was pastor of the First Baptist Church in Jena, Louisiana. It was told to him by senior deacon Isaac Wilbanks, who had been a neighbor to Calvin and Mattie. (Isaac was the father of C. E. Wilbanks, evangelism leader for Mississippi Baptists and later with the Home Mission Board.) Here's the story:

At a summer revival under an arbor, Mattie always sat on the second row of the crude benches. Her husband, Calvin, attended but always stood outside the arbor. As the evangelist gave the invitation one night, Calvin made the decision to accept Christ. Mattie was unaware of his decision until he walked by the bench where she was sitting. When he passed her on the way to the altar, she jumped to her feet, clapped her hands, and exclaimed, "Thank God—there goes 36 years of prayer!"

Although they were living in Pineville at the time, it's most likely they had returned home for the annual brush arbor meeting at Bistineau Baptist Church. Mr. Wilbanks' reference to their attending this same meeting for several summers is proof of such. Too, a brush arbor revival in the town of Pineville would have been more unlikely.

In 1915, as the war clouds of World War I continued to gather in Europe, B. B. McKinney left "lovely" Louisiana to study music at the new Southwestern Baptist Seminary in Fort Worth, Texas, which had opened in 1907. He was now twenty-eight years of age, single, with two hundred revivals under his belt. Still, he was not committed to a church-related career.

His sister Carrie, who so often accompanied him as he sang, later said, "Ben (B. B.) wrote many letters of regret to Mother that he had not stayed in the field of music while Dad was living. It was at the seminary that he made a full surrender to the Lord. I fully believe that Ben was called to this work just as a preacher is called (but) that he fought the call for some time."

McKinney considered this his best work, written while he was at Southwestern Seminary:

Satisfied with Jesus

1. I am sat-is-fied with Je-sus, He has done so much for me:
2. He is with me in my tri-als, Best of friends of all is he;
3. I can hear the voice of Je-sus, Call-ing out so plead-ing-ly,
4. When my work on earth is end-ed, And I cross the mys-tic sea,

He has suf-fered to re-deem me, He has died to set me free.
I can al-ways count on Je-sus, Can he al-ways count on me?
"Go and win the lost and stray-ing;" Is he sat-is-fied with me?
Oh, that I could hear him say-ing, "I am sat-is-fied with thee."

I am sat-is-fied, I am sat-is-fied, I am sat-is-fied with Je-sus, But the ques-tion comes to me, As I think of Cal-va-ry, Is my Mas-ter sat-is-fied with me?

Words and tune ROUTH, B. B. McKinney, 1926. Copyright 1926. Renewed 1953 Broadman Press. All rights reserved.

2
"I Like the Way You Sing"

In the fall of 1915, B. B. McKinney moved to Fort Worth, Texas to enroll in the first class of the new School of Gospel Music at Southwestern Baptist Theological Seminary. Isham E. Reynolds, founder, was the only faculty member. Although he earned no degree, McKinney studied there through 1918. His courses included harmony, music history, conducting, evangelism, history of hymns and their tunes, notation, sight reading, voice, piano, and ensembles. That first year the College Avenue Baptist Church in Fort Worth also employed him as part-time music director.

L. R. Scarborough was president of the seminary, which was housed totally in the new Fort Worth Hall (administration, classes, offices, dormitory, meals, and library).

During my research on this book, I received a letter dated February 2, 1984 from a lady who met B. B. when he arrived on campus that fall. She was Mrs. L. E. (Miriam McConnell) Lamb, 85, of Boiling Springs, North Carolina.

Miriam, a high school senior that year, lived in Fort Worth Hall with her sister, mother, and father, the late F. M. McConnell. Dr. McConnell, a sort of staff evangelist at the seminary, was the next year elected executive secretary of the Baptist General Convention of Oklahoma.

She wrote me:

> Our meals were served family style in the seminary dining room. The same people sat at each table all year. We had the pleasure of Mr. McKinney at ours.
>
> He roomed with L. E. Lamb, later to be my husband, who had come to the seminary from his home in Missouri. He and a young

woman made up the first graduating class in the new music department.

Mr. McKinney wanted a piano in their room, but of course there wasn't space. So to make room for it, they got the idea of putting one bed above the other—you might say they were the first bunk beds ever used!

They put both of the head pieces on the lower bed and both foot pieces on the upper bed. Then they fastened the two beds together, making room for a piano.

As early as then, I remember the seminary choir singing "The Messiah" at Christmas.

As a student McKinney continued to lead singing in revivals, summer assemblies, Baptist conventions, and the like.

Two red-letter events in his student career took place in 1916. That year he published privately, for the first time, a collection of six hymns. (He wrote both words and music for three: "Come Here Today," "Do Something for Jesus Today," and "Let Jesus Have Control." He wrote the music only for three hymn texts by Lizzie Dearmond: "Follow Where Your Saviour Leadeth," "My Saviour's Love," and "Don't Forget Your Precious Mother.")

The second highlight of 1916 occurred on a November afternoon when B. B. was seated on the platform in the First Baptist Church of Waco, Texas. It was the annual convention of the Baptist General Convention of Texas. Seated next to him were Dr. and Mrs. I. E. Reynolds.

Looking over the audience, B. B. spotted Leila Routh, a teacher at Mary Hardin-Baylor College in Belton, Texas. Apparently it was love at first sight, for B. B. turned to Reynolds and said, "You see that girl down there? She's mine if I can ever get her!"

"We know her," the Reynolds replied. "We met her in a revival at her college last month. We'll introduce you." And they did.

B. B. wrote Leila a note that first afternoon which she carried in her purse for years. They were engaged the very next month, in December. "And believe me, I didn't waste much time saying 'Yes,'" she told an audience at Ridgecrest, North Carolina in the summer of 1974. "I didn't want him to change his mind." They were married a year and a half later, on June 11, 1918.

Before they were married, the woman who had meant so much to him during his impressionable years in Louisiana died of pneumonia.

Mattie McKinney passed away shortly after midnight on the morning of June 8, 1917, at the home in Pineville where they'd moved to be near Louisiana College. She was only fifty-eight. B. B. was a month short of being thirty-one.

Her body was shipped by train from nearby Alexandria to Heflin. Carolyn (Davis) McFarland, one of her granddaughters who now lives in Heflin, Louisiana, remembers:

> We were living in the old McKinney place and the railroad passed the farm. We watched it go by. Daddy met the train at the station in Heflin and we put the casket in the south room of the house because it was cooler there and that was before embalming was common. I remember the family sprinkling antiseptic deodorant around the casket at night. Mama—who was pregnant then with Winborn, my brother—wanted to view the body. Some said not to, as there was a superstition that pregnant women shouldn't look at a corpse. But our doctor said it was okay and it did her no harm.

B. B. was there, standing beside "Pick" Coleman, the black hired hand she'd led to Christ. And when the long procession of buggies and cars left for the cemetery, a large contingent of black friends followed on foot.

Two of the original eleven McKinneys were still at home—Carrie and Lawson. So Joanna (McKinney) Davis and her family made the McKinney place their home for the next seven years and looked after Carrie and Lawson. (Joanna was the mother of Winborn Davis, who in the preceding chapter describes the McKinney homestead in detail.)

After seven years the Davis family moved back to their own house nearby and rented the McKinney home.

From 1917 on, when B. B. came home for a visit, he made Joanna's his stopping place. "I have to come see Sis—she's my Mama," he'd answer other relatives who asked him to visit them.

Carolyn (Davis) McFarland, one of Joanna's daughters and a niece of B. B., has vivid memories of those many visits from 1917 until his death in 1952.

"He often stopped for a visit when he had an engagement in the area," Carolyn said. "Each night he came, we'd gather around the organ and sing until bedtime. To understand Ben (B. B.), you must understand he was a tease. He'd do anything to make anyone—especially kids—laugh.

"Mama (Joanna) was very devout and serious along with it. Ben liked to kid her. If I was trying to play the organ, he'd tell me to 'swing it.' Mama would complain, 'Ben, I don't want you telling Carolyn to swing it.' Then he'd grab Mama around the waist and say, 'Come on, Sis, let's waltz.'"

Carolyn describes another incident:

> One time when he was home, we visited a revival at the First Baptist Church in Heflin, where I've gone on and off all my life (although I've lived in fourteen states).
>
> When a convert came forward, our pastor asked, "Do you come by baptism or transfer by letter?" She replied, "I came with my aunt and uncle in a wagon."
>
> Ben thought that was the funniest thing. Later, he'd whisper in Mama's ear, "I came in the wagon with my aunt and uncle." She'd reprimand him: "Now Ben, don't talk like that. They are some of the finest people in all this country."

On another occasion, they visited a revival in a different church. Carolyn recalls:

> We were having sentence prayers, with each person invited to offer a short petition. One person prayed, "Oh, Lord, our little brother he are run away from home. Guide his little feetprint wherever he are."
>
> After that, Mama had to pinch Ben to keep him from whispering that in her ear too. He'd explain, "I'm not making fun of the people themselves."

Carolyn went on to tell me about visiting what she thought was a Baptist church when she lived in Dallas, Texas. Her story gives unusual insight into the wit of B. B. McKinney:

> We visited this church on the invitation of a friend. I took my 3-year-old boy, Ted. When we got home, Ted said, "Mother, that was holy rollies." Later, when we saw Ben (B. B.), he told him the same.
>
> "No, those were funDAMentalist Baptists," Ben replied. Ted answered, "Uncle Ben, you talk ugly. My Mama will preach to you."
>
> Ben then asked, "Why? What did I say that was ugly?"
>
> "You said fun-dam," Ted reminded him.
>
> He'd do anything for a laugh. We thought the world of him. Mama was his second mother—she helped make him what he was, even though she was just his sister.

The year following his mother's death, B. B. was married to Leila Routh, the girl he met at the state convention in Waco, Texas. The date was June 11, 1918, and the place was the home of Leila's mother in Giddings, Texas. "It was a plain country wedding, not a dress-up affair," Mrs. McKinney told me. "I was looking at his face—didn't care what we wore."

World War I was in progress; and the very next month, on July 15, B. B. enlisted in the U.S. Army at Camp Bowie, Texas. After basic training and four weeks of instruction in truck repair and mechanics, he was scheduled to go overseas from Norfolk, Virginia. But when his superiors discovered his musical talent, they kept him at Fort Monroe, Virginia as a sort of morale-booster. The war ended November 11 and he was discharged December 16 at Camp Bowie, after exactly three months of service.

Three doors of opportunity opened for B. B. in 1919. That spring, I. E. Reynolds invited him to join the faculty at Southwestern Seminary as a teacher of voice. Thus began a twelve-year teaching stint at the seminary which lasted until 1931.

The second door was study in Chicago that led to the Bachelor of Music Degree from the Siegel-Myers School of Music in 1922. He took correspondence courses from Siegel-Myers as well as doing resident work during the summers of 1920 and 1921. While in Chicago, he also took some work at Bush Conservatory.

The third door in 1919 was an invitation to join Dallas music publisher Robert Coleman as music editor, a relationship that lasted until 1935.

The 1920s were exciting years for the McKinneys. As William J. Reynolds notes, "His popularity as a teacher and his reputation as a composer and song leader increased steadily. He was in great demand for revivals and summer assemblies. Beginning in 1925 and continuing through 1947, he led the music at Falls Creek Baptist Assembly in Oklahoma. There he became a returning hero each year."

Porter W. Routh, his nephew by marriage, remembers visiting their home on Seminary Hill: "Uncle Mac would show me around the campus. I remember especially the pleasure he found in showing me the new Cowden Music Hall with all the pianos and other materials they had for training musicians."

The 1920s also saw the birth of their two sons—B. B., Jr. on April 4, 1920, and Eugene C. on October 2, 1922.

B. B., Jr. recalls some of those years:

> Seminary Hill was a nice place to grow up. It was a little community in itself, with open spaces between us and Fort Worth. The early streetcar ended its run two blocks from our house, and later a city bus came within a half block.
>
> Before Dad became music director at Travis Avenue Baptist Church in Forth Worth, we attended Seminary Hill Baptist Church (now Gambrell Street). Dad was ordained a deacon there in 1920.
>
> I remember Dad as a quiet man. He'd be off in his room, writing, then come out to the piano, pick out a melody, polish it, add the chords. He didn't play the piano and didn't use it to compose, but did pick around.
>
> Mother had little natural talent for music, but she studied piano out of sheer perseverance, to help Dad. She tried to teach both me and Gene to play, but had little success.

At age 11, I got a trombone and played in the school orchestra. I fell in love with it. One of my first teachers was Don Gillis, who went on to a 25-year-career with NBC. Hardin-Simmons University gave me a scholarship for playing in the Cowboy Band.

Although Dad didn't have a trained voice (he would never have made it in opera!), his voice was powerful and he sang with feeling. The emotion of it all touched me as a boy. He was mainly a composer and congregational song leader, not a soloist.

I never saw Dad really upset or even raise his voice in anger. He wasn't a worrier. He was at peace with himself, doing what he loved. He could be tough with a strap, then hug me. But he disciplined without anger.

I was 16 when we moved from Seminary Hill to Nashville. I remember the coal smoke and the wet winters in Nashville, but I liked it.

Eugene also recalls Seminary Hill, the close-knit community that included the campus, some residences, a church or two, and a post office:

I remember Seminary Hill as a boy because of the open spaces where you could play. However, we avoided "Bull Dog" Crowder who was in charge of the grounds.

Dad had a morning routine. He'd shave, dress, and walk a block to the post office, where he'd visit until breakfast was ready. Back then, the post office on Seminary Hill was a social center. No one was a stranger to him. He wasn't what you'd call an extrovert, but he did have tremendous interest in people—from kids to wealthy adults.

I remember him telling about a revival in a country church. He was at a farmer's home for dinner. They were out in the pigpen when the farmer asked, "I know you're Dr. McKinney, but can I call you B. B.?" The next day, Dad lunched with W. R. White, president of Baylor University. He was equally and comfortably at home with both men.

Dad had a great love for the soil. He was a good gardener. At one time he rented a couple of empty lots for this purpose. That was about 1932 to 1934.

Gene also remembers early impressions of his father as a composer and his work habits:

> He was gone a lot. When he'd come home, he smelled of cigar and coal smoke from the trains. He always brought us a little gift or memento from the city he'd visited.
>
> He didn't have an office at home. But he could sit down in a big overstuffed chair, with a sheet of plywood across the arms for a desk, while streams of teenagers ran through the house. He'd just keep writing—occasionally look up and smile.
>
> His concentration was tremendous. He could have worked at a busy, noisy intersection if someone had barricaded him a work space!
>
> During those years, he was under contract to Robert Coleman for so many choruses and songs a year. One time he got behind and went to the Davis Mountains for a week by himself—then came home with 20 compositions he'd written or edited.
>
> He could write a new chorus during a sermon. I could tell when he was composing for he'd start whistling silently to himself. He'd purse his lips just so. The stimulus of the moment gave him his ideas for songs.
>
> One time I witnessed him write both the words and music during a service, hand the score to the pianist, then sing it.
>
> I remember him as tall and magnificent as he stood on a platform at church or a convention, his arms uplifted. He could beat me at arm-wrestling when I was in high school. He loved good clothes—laymen often bought him a new suit during a revival. He kept his shoes shined and spotless and expected the same of us.
>
> We had lots of company and he enjoyed good food. After dinner, he'd say, "Take me out but don't bend me." I've heard him say that a hundred times.
>
> In the early 1950s he told my playwriting class at Baylor, "I

view myself as a working artist, not a religious worker for the denomination."

The following note gives insight into his role as an evangelistic singer during those years. It was hand-written from Middlesboro, Kentucky on stationery of the Lowry Hotels. The date and name of the church and pastor are missing. He described a revival which saw sixty-seven conversions one Sunday morning, forty-two of them men:

> I made the call in the men's class. 42 came. John L. Hill's brother is the teacher, one of the grandest men I ever met. I sang the Pilgrim song in the old minor key and I never saw a crowd so broken up. Hill asked me to make the call. The chief of police was in the number that came. This is the highest day for Christ I have ever had. Tell Reynolds about it and ask my classes to pray for us.

Then he added greetings to his family, the first sentence telling us that Mrs. McKinney probably looked after the practical side of things:

> Glad the screens are repaired. Wish I could tell you how much I love you, but that can never be written down. I am real lonesome for you all. Kiss the dear, sweet boys for me and tell them I love them heaps and heaps. God bless you all, sweet babies o'mine. Love and kisses, your own Dad.

Seminary president L. R. Scarborough, himself an effective evangelist, wrote B. B. on July 24, 1922 from Lampasas, Texas:

> We are having a great time. We leave here next Saturday. Will get home Saturday night. I go from there about the 4th or 5th to Gainesville, Georgia. I wish we could be together in another meeting. Hope we can soon. I like you. I like the way you sing and the way you handle the crowd. I don't know of any big, raw-boned sinner I love more than I do you. Yesterday, Ike sang with the crowd your two songs—"Carry Your Burden With a Smile" and "He Lives on High"—I said to a big denominational leader that those two songs would immortalize anybody; and he said he agreed with me.

The following letter from C. S. Hodge of Waynesville, North Carolina, illustrates B. B.'s organizational genius with volunteer choirs. His letter is dated January 30, 1984:

> I think the first time I met him was the summer of 1927 when I enrolled in his class at Southwestern. There was a quiet magnetism about his leading that just made folks want to sing, and to sing like he suggested.
>
> One summer during my stay at Southwestern, we held a city-wide revival under a big tent. George W. Truett was the preacher and Ike Reynolds led the singing. They asked Dr. McKinney and me to organize the choir of some 800 voices. At least I know it was in the hundreds.
>
> He and I contacted all the Baptist churches in the county for names of their choir members. We divided the choir into voice sections, then numbered each seat. We assigned seats to the singers and had a waiting list. The choir was full every night, as well as the big circus-like tent that seated two or three thousand. Dr. Scarborough trained the soul-winners. Mrs. Reynolds and Mrs. McKinney played the two pianos. It was one of those meetings you don't forget.

I was pleased at the number of letters I received from former students of Mr. McKinney. "I'm past ninety," wrote Pearl Farr of Orlando, Florida. "But I remember that B. B. and my husband, Theodore H. Farr, graduated in the same class in 1919. Each sang solo parts in *The Messiah* at Christmas. Both were of a jolly nature and when they got together, there was hilarity. B. B. nearly broke up the seminary choir one day when a young man came down the aisle wearing reddish-brown shoes. B. B. said, so all could hear, 'Here comes two red shoats down the lane!'"

And from Toccoa, Georgia came a letter from Ira F. McMinn, who roomed in the McKinney home for a year: "No finer man could have been found for a music teacher. I never knew him to be upset about anything."

Tommie Godfrey of Tyler, Texas will never forget B. B. McKinney, one of the first persons Tommie met when he arrived on campus in 1929 with $1.45 in his pockets. He continues:

I didn't have enough money to bring my family on the bus, so I hitchhiked to Fort Worth. B. B. recognized my predicament. He would just happen along at the right time when I needed help. He saw that my Model T had enough gas to make it to Travis Avenue Church, where I was soloist for the Travis Avenue Vespers on radio. I sang many of his songs in manuscript form before they were published. He often helped us with food.

Later I was general music director for the Alto Frio Encampment in the hills north of Uvalde, Texas, the largest in the state. So I asked them to get B. B. for the congregational singing—he had no equal.

Mildred Seay of Baton Rouge, Louisiana remembers going to the seminary as a fourteen-year-old when her dad enrolled as a student. Her mother, Maggie Money, accompanied B. B. when he gave voice lessons. She adds, "Sometimes they'd practice at our house, and it went on so long that during my senior year in high school, I hardly had time or quiet to study."

William G. Stroup of Jacksonville, Florida says B. B. taught him sight reading by the "solfege system." Textbooks often consisted of mimeographed copies of lessons B. B. had written. After the new *Modern Hymnal* came out in 1926, B. B. used it in class since it had a number of his songs and choruses. Mr. Stroup adds:

> My first Sunday in Fort Worth, I. E. Reynolds asked me to sing a solo at Broadway Baptist Church. I sang a number called "Others," which I'd discovered early in my youth at the Presbyterian church of our little town. I sang it several times and when B. B. heard it, he asked for a copy. In 1940, he published it on page 77 of *The Broadman Hymnal*.

Marian (Bossemeyer) Goff wrote me from Dallas, saying she and her mother lived next door to the McKinneys the first year Marian studied at the seminary. "Often I was at the McKinney home when Mr. Mac came in from school. If he'd written a new song that day, he wanted to hear how it sounded. So I'd play it. Many of those efforts went into the wastebasket, but I was thrilled to be the first to play them, whatever their merit."

Milton S. Leach, Jr. of Fort Lauderdale, Florida prizes a mimeographed copy of evangelistic choruses by McKinney, published in 1923 while he was a teacher at the seminary. "Many of those choruses I learned from Brother McKinney when, as a small boy, I attended the Alto Frio Baptist Encampment and surrendered my life for special service. I've been a missionary for thirty-eight years."

Another McKinney student was Norvell Slater, whose Sunday morning broadcasts of sacred music on radio WFAA in Dallas have, for years, thrilled thousands of listeners. "Mr. McKinney was more than a capable harmony teacher—he was a warm friend," Slater said. "He often spoke of Stephen Foster's incredible ability to compose melodies that were singable, catchy, and easy to remember. B. B. possessed that same God-given talent. To me, his name is almost synonymous with Baptist music. We often rode the same trolley and sat together and talked. . . ."

After nearly sixty years as an evangelistic singer, Joe Trussell of Brownwood, Texas recalled the years of 1921-24 at Southwestern under McKinney: "He helped establish priorities and attitudes which I've tried to observe."

Then in twelve words, Trussell summed it all: "Perhaps I should say that the Lord inspired him to inspire me."

Others wrote:

"I met him in the fall of 1919 when I enrolled at Southwestern. He took an abiding interest in me. As our friendship grew, he encouraged me to write sacred music. He was generous in his praise"—H. P. Black, Longview, Texas.

"I drove 30 miles to Ft. Worth, three days a week, to attend his classes. To me, that was a lifelong thrill to my soul"—Taylor F. McCasland, Lubbock, Texas.

"Mr. McKinney inspired his students in every way. Male quartets were popular then. My husband, Herbert, sang in the seminary quartet along with Ellis Carnett, McKinney, and Leonard Perkins. Leonard and Herbert were students, for Mr. McKinney used students whenever he could. Once when Herbert was going out in a revival, Mr. McKinney gave him a copy of a new song, 'Let Others See Jesus in You.' He said to take it along and see if it was singable. Of course it was. And Herbert was always pleased for the opportunity to help introduce it"—Stella F. Findley, Chula Vista, California.

McKinney wrote some of his best-loved hymns during the 1920s and early 1930s.* Here are thirteen of them:

> Satisfied with Jesus
> The Nail-Scarred Hand
> 'Neath the Old Olive Trees
> All on the Altar
> Serve the Lord with Gladness
> Speak to My Heart
> Have Faith in God
> Send a Great Revival
> Let Others See Jesus in You
> I Know the Bible Is True
> Wherever He Leads I'll Go

The third door that opened to McKinney in 1919 was an offer to be part-time music editor for Dallas publisher Robert H. Coleman. This relationship lasted until 1935.

The joint venture was good for both men. It disciplined McKinney to finalize his own compositions for publication. It also gave him further exposure in the churches which bought Coleman's hymnals. And of course, Coleman benefited from McKinney's editing skills, as well as his popularity throughout the South and Southwest.

In his book *Wherever He Leads I'll Go*, Paul R. Powell claims that before McKinney went to the Baptist Sunday School Board in 1935, practically all of his published hymns appeared in Coleman's collections. Powell says

---

*McKinney ordinarily didn't sit down on a given day and write and copyright a piece. He might write the chorus and sing it here and there, adding verses later. So to determine actual date of composition, it is safe to predate most of the copyright notices.

that 261 of McKinney's works were published between 1916 and 1935—moreover, that 230 of the 261 were published by Coleman.

A letter from Coleman on November 25, 1925 reveals their informal working agreement:

> I am sending this by special delivery to make sure you receive it Thursday morning, with the hope you may promptly get the proofs off to Chicago as early Thursday as possible.
>
> I presume this is the last proof I will send you, as there are only two more songs and they are reprints. I will instruct Anderson to turn over the plates to Conley on Saturday or as soon as your revised proofs get back to him.
>
> We had no financial understanding about your work, but I am enclosing you my check for $100, merely for your proofreading and other assistance. I presume you would not charge so much, but I am glad to pay it and wish it were more. I owe you for the songs, and the first time I see you and we can go over the matter, I will give you a check for that.
>
> I love you as a brother, I appreciate you as a friend, and I esteem you as a gifted and capable musician. With tenderest devotions, I am, cordially, Robert H. Coleman.

In his book *The Songs of B.B. McKinney,* William J. Reynolds says that during the years he and McKinney worked together, 1919-1935, Coleman published twenty-nine songbooks, all of which contained some songs by McKinney. Better known ones were *The Modern Hymnal* (1926) and *The American Hymnal* (1933).

Coleman himself is an interesting person. Born in Bardstown, Kentucky in 1869, he came to Texas in 1888 to open a drugstore in Plano, Texas.

He moved to Dallas in 1901 as assistant secretary of the Y.M.C.A., where he lived until his death in 1946.

He joined the First Baptist Church in Dallas and served as the pastor's assistant for forty-three years (1903-46). Although never ordained, he assisted pastor George W. Truett in funerals, prayer services, administration, and visitation. He was a deacon the same number of years, and

Sunday School superintendent for thirty-six years. Best of all, he enjoyed leading congregational singing, which he did in his own church as well as state conventions, the Southern Baptist Convention, and the Baptist World Alliance. Known widely as "Brother Bob," he had a keen insight into what Baptists liked to sing.

For thirty-seven years, he edited and published songbooks, selling more than thirteen million copies of thirty-three different hymnals. One hymnal sold nearly 100,000 copies a year for twenty years. Another stayed in print for thirty years.

The February 21, 1946 issue of *The Baptist Standard* refers to him as "the largest individual publisher of song books in the country."

McKinney edited for Coleman not only while he was on the faculty, but for four years after he left Southwestern.

Why did McKinney leave Southwestern in 1931? It depends on who you talk to. Some say he left because the seminary couldn't afford to pay him during the Great Depression. Others say it was conflict between him and I. E. Reynolds. Perhaps there is some truth in both claims.

Inman Johnson, retired faculty member at Southern Baptist Theological Seminary in Louisville, Kentucky, was on the staff of the first music week at Ridgecrest Baptist Conference Center. For two summers he roomed with McKinney. "Reynolds and McKinney had a ruckus," Johnson wrote me.

J. D. Grey, retired pastor of the First Baptist Church in New Orleans, was with McKinney at Falls Creek Baptist Assembly, plus a number of revivals. Grey wrote me:

> It's a known secret around Southwestern Seminary that a conflict developed between I. E. Reynolds, head of the school of music, and McKinney over the type music that ought to be used. Reynolds insisted on the more stately hymns as some would call "long-haired" music, but McKinney was a strong one for Gospel music. Well, the conflict got so bad that one day President Scarborough called McKinney into his office and said, "Brother Ben, you know I love you. I admire you very much. But in the conflict between you and Ike, I don't see any reconciliation possible. So I

think you had better seek another place and let us go with Ike as head of the school of music."

In his book *Wherever He Leads I'll Go,* Paul R. Powell acknowledges "tension" between the two professors. He says the tension was "a difference in philosophy" about church music. Powell says after professor Albert Venting returned to Southwestern from England, he brought a "high church" emphasis that Reynolds came to favor. However, Powell concludes that McKinney left over economic necessity, not personalities.

In his book *The Songs of B. B. McKinney,* William J. Reynolds says the seminary was in dire financial straits in the summer of 1931. When President Scarborough told I. E. Reynolds the music faculty must be cut by one, he also asked his advice over who should be terminated. Rather than lose one of his teachers, Reynolds turned in his own resignation.

William Reynolds goes on to say that Dr. Scarborough then informed the other music faculty of I. E. Reynolds' action. Shortly, all three (McKinney, Ellis Carnett, and Edwin McNeely) resigned, too. After prayer and careful study, Scarborough accepted McKinney's resignation, feeling McKinney could best survive. His reasoning was that McKinney was already part-time music director at Travis Avenue Baptist Church, an associate with publisher Robert Coleman, and in wide demand as an evangelistic and convention song leader.

Clifford A. Holcomb, retired staff member of the Church Music Department at the Baptist Sunday School Board, furnished me a lengthy analysis, based on conversations with all four of the faculty persons, plus his own working relationship with McKinney. Holcomb told me that he had been told that Mrs. McKinney said, "Reynolds got McKinney fired from the seminary." Holcomb emphasized to me that this was second-hand information.

Here is Holcomb's analysis:

1. Scarborough made the final decision as to which of the four should leave. All four volunteered to do so.

2. Reynolds and McKinney did disagree. Reynolds was a strong advocate of English hymnody. McKinney emphasized the gospel song form.

3. In later years, Reynolds was disappointed that the Baptist Sunday School Board chose McKinney to head the music department in Nashville. "I don't believe Reynolds ever wanted the job, but he didn't believe McKinney to be the proper one," Holcomb told me.

4. Throughout, there was no hatred by either man. Holcomb thinks the rumor was fed by some Fort Worth area pastors whom Reynolds had severely criticized for their lack of music standards. Holcomb thinks these pastors were hitting back at Reynolds and using the McKinney incident as a platform.

Holcomb also told me that McKinney and Reynolds were in Jacksonville, Florida in January 1947 for an associational music school. Holcomb said he loved both men and regretted this misunderstanding. So he arranged adjoining rooms for them in the Seminole Hotel and opened the doors between. "During the week they had lots of time together," Holcomb said. "Both men told me later that this was the first time they had been together in many years under circumstances favorable for talking. Each told me they reached an understanding, had renewed their friendship, and had no animosity toward the other."

I'm indebted to Clifford Holcomb for an additional insight as to what happened in 1931. A few days after McKinney resigned, he ran into J. Frank Norris downtown. Norris was pastor of the First Baptist Church in Fort Worth, an independent fundamentalist who repeatedly criticized the seminary, as well as Southern Baptists in general.

Reportedly, Norris said, "Ben, they tell me they cut you off the faculty."

McKinney replied by doubling up his fist and putting it right up against Norris' mouth. In so many words, he said, "Frank, if you say one word about this over your radio, I'll stick this fist right down your big mouth, reach down inside you, and turn you inside out."

Holcomb was told that Norris never mentioned the issue either on radio or in his church.

And so classes opened at Southwestern in September of 1931 without McKinney in the classrooms where he'd taught since 1919. He was now forty-five and riding the crest of his popularity as a "platform man" who knew how to get people to sing and to enjoy it as well.

But he left Seminary Hill, according to Porter W. Routh, knowing that some had criticized him for being "just a congregational song leader."

Some song leader! Some congregations!

This popular gospel song reflects the strong emphasis on evangelism which characterized the Matthews-McKinney years at Travis Avenue Baptist Church:

Send a Great Revival

3
"Sometimes I'd Hold His Hand"

Throughout his 1915-1931 career at Southwestern Baptist Seminary, both as a student and a professor, B. B. McKinney wore many hats. For example, in 1915-16, he served as music director at the College Avenue Baptist Church in Fort Worth. In the summer of 1925 he began a twenty-two-year stint as music director at Falls Creek Baptist Assembly in Oklahoma. Sometime during this period he started leading the singing at the famed "cowboy encampment" near Paisano, Texas, where George W. Truett preached each summer.

In 1919 he started working part-time for Robert Coleman. And in late 1928 the Travis Avenue Baptist Church employed both B. B. and Mrs. McKinney on a part-time paid basis. He directed the music and she served as Training Union director.

Pastor C. E. Matthews wrote in the December 13, 1928 church newsletter:

> Brother McKinney needs no introduction to Baptists anywhere in the South. He is professor of music in the Southwestern Seminary, nationally known as a song writer of sacred music, a soloist of note and without a peer as a director of choir and congregational music. The moment he steps on a platform to sing, it seems he creates by his appearance and manner a genuine reverence. . . . Travis Avenue has long wished for Bro. McKinney to be our music leader. We thank God now that he is one of us. Let's build a choir of 117 voices! We have the seats for them.

When McKinney resigned from Southwestern Seminary in 1931, Travis Avenue employed him full-time. He and his family continued to live at

4504 Frazier near the seminary, and he kept an office on campus where he taught private lessons.

Apparently the decision to cut back on the music faculty was made late in 1930, for on January 8, 1931, McKinney wrote in the Travis Avenue newsletter:

> My heart sings with joy as I come to this great church for fulltime work. I join heart and hand with our beloved pastor and all others in making Travis Avenue Church a lighthouse for drifting, sinking, drowning souls. . . . My office and studio is in Barnard Hall, where I shall spend much of my time teaching private voice, conducting, and sight singing. We plan to reorganize the choir (Travis Avenue) to keep all seats filled. A men's chorus will be organized next Sunday. I hope the orchestra will be the largest and best to be found anywhere. I am also coming to help Bro. Matthews with the men. We are praying that God will help us win many men to Him this year.

In his book *Wherever He Leads I'll Go,* Paul R. Powell said that since Dr. Matthews "detested anthems and anything else that suggested formality in worship," he and McKinney worked well together. Powell quotes R. H. York, who sang in the Travis Avenue choir and recalls that although McKinney held rehearsals, attendance was not required. Any who wished to sing simply walked up and sat down in the choir loft before the service.

Warren M. Angell, who later knew McKinney at Oklahoma Baptist University, told me that in the old auditorium in use at the time, the choir loft was circular. It had ten tiers of seats—actually benches—arranged in a circular, radiating style. Angell added that today, choirs often sit in straight rows, so that singers on the ends can't hear the others. Angell said he understood the Sunday night choirs often numbered in the hundreds.

Roland Leath of Shelby, North Carolina wrote me that for four years, he played one of the pianos for the worship services, while Mrs. McKinney played the other:

> Often during the services Mr. McKinney would reach inside his coat pocket for a piece of music paper and proceed to write the

notes and words for a "chorus." One Sunday he brought the piece of paper to me and said, "Let's teach them this," and it was the chorus of *Have Faith in God*.

During this time, I surrendered to the call to be a music and educational director. I tried to absorb all I could of the spirit of B. B. McKinney. In his calm, unassuming way he was a blessing and a tower of strength to all of us. One day I asked, "How do you know which songs to select for a service?" He replied, "Long ago I was in a revival and asked the preacher what songs he wanted me to use. The preacher then pointed to a grove of trees and said, 'That's where I get my sermons; go there and get your songs.' From that time, I've just asked the Lord what songs to use."

Mrs. O. D. Sanders of Waco, Texas remembers when she and Mr. Sanders moved to Fort Worth and joined Travis Avenue Church in 1939. McKinney greeted them that morning and invited them to join the choir. They declined, but Mrs. Sanders couldn't say no when Mrs. McKinney telephoned to ask her to serve as director of primary children in Training Union. When Mrs. Sanders said she couldn't, Mrs. McKinney merely said, "I'll see you at the director's meeting," and hung up. Mrs. Sanders says that she went!

When the McKinneys moved from Fort Worth in late 1935 and couldn't sell their house, the Sanders rented it for a few months. Norman H. Sanders of Roanoke, Texas, one of their sons, recalls when Travis Avenue Church was sponsoring a Scoutmaster training program for Boy Scouts. "Dad was a World War I navy veteran and knew how to tie all kinds of sailor knots," Norman wrote me. "One thing he could not do was sing. It turned out that Brother Mac had trouble tying his shoes. So he told Dad, 'Jack, you tie the knots and I'll do the singing!'"

Irene Redford, who is now Mrs. Kenneth C. Phillips of Granbury, Texas, grew up in Travis Avenue Church. She could hardly wait to graduate from high school so she could sing in the adult choir. Irene wrote me:

I was in close contact with the McKinneys for about eight years. I studied piano under Mrs. McKinney and was in their home a lot. One thing he said impressed me very much—that he let the Lord lead in his selection of hymns for Sunday services. He didn't consult with Bro. Matthews about his sermon subjects, but the hymns always carried out the theme of the sermon as if they had been planned.

Many times I've seen him write in a notebook he carried in his pocket, composing a lyric. I sang in the Travis Girl's Trio. At the dedication of our first educational unit, we sang *Have Faith in God*. One of my treasures is his famous autograph he gave me when he left for Nashville in 1935:

Both McKinneys liked and encouraged young people. Betty Ruth Alexander, who still lives in Fort Worth and whose maiden name was Wetzel, came there with her parents in 1939 when her father took violin and voice at the seminary. "At Travis Avenue," she wrote me, "the Juniors (ages 9-12) sat in the balcony and it was his delight to call on one of the children to sing alone. He called on my younger sister, said he loved to hear her sing. He knew *all* the children and was always encouraging them." She also remembers:

> Since it was during the Depression, the young people had to get their fun any way they could. Bro. Mac saw to it that we had lots of fun. He would load several cars and drive us out to the country, build a big fire, fill the coffee pot, and we'd gather around and sing and talk. At the close, he would get serious and spoke of spiritual things and gave us love and encouragement.

Petty says the nicest gift she ever received was a high school graduation ring, paid for by friends at the church. "Lou Williams Crotts, one of the secretaries, kept a little box on her desk and invited anyone to contribute nickels and dimes for my ring, and to sign their name. Mr. and Mrs. McKinney gave a dinner for the choir officers at their home and presented me with the ring. I still wear it, after 50 years. And Mrs. McKinney paid my way to my first state Training Union convention. We went by bus and what fun! She was clever."

About 1981, many of the youth whom the McKinneys befriended held a reunion. Calling themselves the "Travis Gang," they flew Mrs. McKinney to Fort Worth for the occasion. She knew every one of them, although nearly fifty years had passed.

Each summer the McKinneys helped plan a church youth camp. William D. Swank of Fort Worth has his mother's diary that describes the 1933 camp. His mother, Elizabeth McClure, who attended the camp, was at the time engaged to Fred Swank, the youthful pastor of the Sagamore Hill Baptist Church in Fort Worth. He had already given her a ring and they were to be married in 1934. Here's her entry on July 14, 1933:

> Led sunrise prayer meeting. Met with discipline committee all morning. Sent Edna and Pauline home. Had good decision service. Bro. Mac let Fred and I stay out to 11:15. We had a rather frank talk.

By 1936, when Elizabeth was the pastor's wife at Sagamore Hill Church, she took a Sunday School class on a summer retreat. And in 1940, the church began its own Camp Sagamore, patterned after Camp Travis. In the summer of 1983 William Swank wrote me, "Next month our church will hold its 43rd youth camp, and I feel sure that B. B. McKinney would feel right at home if he were there."

Some old correspondence from 1931 and 1932 reveals more of McKinney's faith in young people.

One is a four-page, handwritten letter, dated May 30, 1932, which McKinney wrote to Fred Swank just as he was graduating from Simmons (now Hardin-Simmons) University in Abilene. He said he was writing as "your Big Brother in Christ." Among other things, he said a Christian worker fails:

—When he puts Christ second.
—When he has little time to study God's Word and pray.

—When he has no confidence in himself or his fellowman.

—When he values success more than self-respect.

—When he lets a day go by without speaking to someone about Christ or making someone happier.

—When he lets the victory song die out of his heart.

—When he ignores the advice of his friends, stops to take counsel with an enemy, or knows he's in the wrong but won't admit it.

B. B. McKinney saved very little of his own correspondence or letters he received from others. In fact, my research found not a single carbon copy of any of his correspondence during the years he headed the Church Music Department at the Baptist Sunday School Board. For one thing, he often wrote his letters in longhand, with no carbon copies.

But one letter he did save is dated April 28, 1931. It was written by Troupe Reid, who had grown up in Travis Avenue Church and was then a student at Baylor University in Waco, Texas with no financial support.

The same day, W. A. Criswell, now of Dallas, wrote McKinney from Waco. Criswell and Troupe roomed in the home of a Mrs. Rogers, a widow. Criswell wrote McKinney how the week before, he had found a Bible "in the study chair" in Troupe's room. It was open to the promise, "If ye have faith as a grain of mustard seed, nothing shall be impossible unto you. . . ." Under the Bible was a letter from Baylor's cashier, warning, "We are asking that you come immediately and clear the $24 debt you owe the University for the Spring Quarter."

Criswell noted in his letter that "if Troupe had over a dollar, it was news to me."

Not long after, Criswell notes, "Troupe came into my room with a letter from Big Brother Mac, and in that letter was $30!" And Troupe wrote McKinney:

> Bro. Mac, I was praying for a way to open, but my prayer was to open up a way 'for me to make my own way,' when your check came. It seemed more like a fairy story than a reality. To say I thank you would be too mild. It took almost an hour to cry it out!

After graduating from Baylor, Troupe Reid married the youth director from Travis Avenue, whose first name was Pauline. Troupe died soon afterward, which probably accounts for why McKinney kept his letter.

Another evidence of McKinney's love for young people was frequent visits to the Buckner Orphan's Home in Dallas (now Buckner Baptist Benevolences). I received several letters from persons who lived at the Home in the 1930s and even 1940s, and remember McKinney's visits. Apparently, he continued to visit the campus after leaving Texas in 1935.

Ruth Mims Taylor wrote me from Denison, Texas:

> My husband, Gordon, was dean of boys at Buckner for 12 years. During those years, Bro. McKinney led the singing for summer revivals. The children—some seven hundred of them then—adored "Big Brother," as they fondly called him. He had such a winning personality and his singing caused many to find Christ.

From Dallas, Dessie Hamrick wrote me that she lived at the home in the 1940s: "During the summers on some hot Sunday afternoons he would lead what we called Sing-Alongs. There were some good times and I will always treasure them."

Irene Farris Cagle of Houston, who was reared in the Home, said, "We all loved him so much and when he was leading, we would sing better and louder for him than anyone."

Mrs. McKinney said their phone often rang and a voice would ask, "Is Big Brother there?" She knew it was one of the Buckner boys or girls, passing through Fort Worth, wanting to talk. "Those kids loved him," she said. "I'd drive out there and leave him for a week during the summer. They clung to him, adored him. Filled a need in their lives; taught them songs. On the days to leave, the children would gather around our car. The staff would have to clear the way before I could drive away."

Faye (Calvert) Conant of Marble Falls, Texas lived at the Home, 1925-31. "I can still remember some of the songs we sang," she wrote me. "And he would also sing for us. I wish I had a recording of him singing, "Those Golden Bells." How he could make them ring! I count it a rare privilege to have known him. I'm glad I lived there and had a chance to finish high school."

Mrs. C. C. Evans of San Marcos, Texas remembers the years she lived there as a little girl, 1930-39. "We all called him Big Brother, for he said that's what B. B. meant," she wrote me. "When he came, we all sang:

> Big Brother's here,
> Big Brother's here.
> Everybody's happy
> Because Big Brother's here.

One of the most touching letters came from Faye (Elder) Owens. She is a half-sister to Lloyd Elder, now president of the Baptist Sunday School Board in Nashville.

Her mother, the former Emma Dagley, died in March of 1926 following childbirth. She left eight children, ages two to fourteen. The father, Joseph E. Elder, was ill himself and unable to care for them. He talked with L. R. Scarborough, a member of the board at Buckner Orphan's Home. Joseph had met Scarborough when he was a student at Southwestern Seminary. Scarborough helped place five of the Elder children in the Home. The older ones stayed with their Dad.

Faye picks up the story:

> The next thing, five frightened little kids left their home in Patton, Texas for Buckners. I was five. It was agreed we wouldn't be adopted out, but that Daddy could get us anytime, day or night.
>
> For the first two weeks, we stayed in a big two-story house to be sure we didn't have anything "catching." Oh, what a heartache. They put my two little brothers and me in one building, and our older sisters in another. We could visit them only on Sundays. My brothers and I were around strangers, so we cried a lot. Just as we would get settled down, we'd see our sisters in the lunch room and start crying again. My brothers did better, but I was a "Daddy's girl." I'd cry just seeing his feet as he walked by the basement window where our Sunday School class was meeting. Every Sunday, I'd cry through my Daddy's whole visit, for I knew he'd have to leave again.

In her letter to me, dated April 12, 1984, Faye goes on to say that one of her vivid memories is "the visits B. B. McKinney made with his sack of candy. Maybe all the children didn't feel as I did—maybe he just filled the place of my Daddy. All I know is, we all loved him. Sometimes I'd get to hold his hand as he and a bunch of us little kids took walks. It's been 58 years ago and I still remember it as if it were yesterday."

The Elder children stayed at Buckner's only two months, but long enough for McKinney to make a lifelong impression. Their father remarried in 1928, giving the original children five more brothers and two stepbrothers.

The fourteenth of the fifteen Elder children was Lloyd, now president of the Baptist Sunday School Board. In a July 20, 1983 interview in the Texas *Baptist Standard,* Lloyd said: "The Elder family was a proud, poor, God-fearing Baptist family and always on the move. By the time I was eight years old, our family had moved through 24 states, working and living in every way possible. I learned how to read from the Burma Shave Signs along the highways."

Meanwhile, McKinney was a familiar figure in conventions, revivals, and assemblies. Orine Hughes Suffern, later a professor of music at Golden Gate Baptist Seminary in California, remembers going to the summer encampments in Texas with her preacher-father. "Many times, during my teens, I was asked to play the piano when Dr. McKinney was leading the music or singing solos," she wrote me. "The most vivid remembrance is his compassion for the lost and needy as he would sing, 'I Am a Poor Wayfaring Stranger' or 'There Is a Balm in Gilead,' with tears rolling down his cheeks."

After McKinney's death in 1952, G. S. Hopkins wrote his widow from Dallas about how he had "relied on B. B., Bob Coleman and Bob Jolly for our Sunday School Convention music." He described the April 14, 1931 convention in Abilene, when some advised him not to go ahead with it because of the Great Depression.

"The morning the convention opened," he recalled, "Bob Jolly was at the piano, B. B. and Bob Coleman were leading the singing. The first song was 'When the Saints Go Marching In.' I dare say there was not a dry eye in the convention hall. Dr. R. C. Pender was heard to say that he had attended Baptist conventions for 50 years and this was the most spiritual he had ever attended. These three giant musicians have (since) all gone marching in. . . ."

B. B.'s fame as a congregational song leader grew. Many came to see, as

Clifford A. Holcomb so aptly describes, that "He could get more singing out of a congregation with the wiggle of a finger than I can, or anyone else, with all the windmill waving in the world."

And when he was invited, for the first time, to lead the singing at the 1932 Southern Baptist Convention in St. Petersburg, Florida, the *Ft. Worth Star-Telegram* described it as "the greatest tribute to his musical talent."

In the seven years that he was on the staff of Travis Avenue Church (two years part-time, five years full-time), he and pastor C. E. Matthews held scores of revivals "in churches of every size scattered over the Southern Baptist Convention territory."

Following McKinney's death in 1952, Matthews wrote for the Baptist state papers:

> Time and again I've seen him sing people into the Kingdom. Once in Sherman, Texas, where the evangelist had given up because of no response, Brother McKinney began singing, 'I Will Arise and Go to Jesus.' When he had finished, 18 grown men had come forward accepting Christ.
>
> His very presence in an assembly was so stimulating that a deacon once said, "B. B. McKinney would be worth his salary if he did nothing but stand on the rostrum."
>
> He stood in the breach for Southern Baptists for 35 years, steering us clear of empty jazz music on one side and liturgical music that leads to cold, dead formalism on the other side.

Meanwhile, forces were at work that would soon thrust McKinney from his warm, person-centered ministry at Travis Avenue Church to Nashville, Tennessee, where he'd become the first head of Southern Baptists' Church Music Department.

The earliest and possibly the strongest force in that direction had been set in motion years earlier by Dr. Isham E. Reynolds, the man who recruited McKinney as a faculty member at Southwestern Seminary in 1919.

In a chapel message at Southwestern Seminary on September 20, 1979, William J. Reynolds quoted Floyd H. Patterson to the effect that Dr. Reynolds "championed the cause of church music among Southern Baptists as did no other of his time."

The chapel message also referred to the 1925 Southern Baptist Convention in Memphis, where Dr. Reynolds presented a resolution asking for the appointment of a committee. Such committee would "report at the next Convention such recommendation as it may deem wise and proper for the advancement of music in the Southern Baptist Convention." Reynolds was named chairman of the committee, which reported to the 1926 Convention in Houston, Texas. Among other things, the committee urged the Convention to "instruct the Sunday School Board to give careful consideration at its earliest convenience to the advisability of establishing and fostering a Church Music Department for the purpose of improving the musical conditions in the stated church, Sunday School, and B.Y.P.U. services of the various churches."

William J. Reynolds said that Dr. Reynolds spoke that same fall at the Texas State Baptist Convention, urging a church music department in the denomination as well as in states.

His 1926 resolution, which was referred to the Sunday School Board, died when I. J. Van Ness analyzed the overall operations of the Board and the decision was that "no new departments would be inaugurated at the present time."

Paul R. Powell writes that a similar effort failed at the 1933 meeting of the Southern Baptist Convention.

The turning point came in early 1935 when T. L. Holcomb was named executive-secretary of the Sunday School Board. A church music editor was one of the first staff members Dr. Holcomb added, and that editor turned out to be B. B. McKinney. Prior to this, the Board had done no music publishing. Instead, it relied on others for the editing and printing of such titles as *The New Baptist Hymnal* in 1926 and *Songs of Faith* in 1933.

How does one account for Holcomb's interest in leadership and music materials for Southern Baptist churches? *The Sunday School Board: Ninety Years of Service* by Walter B. Shurden gives part of the answer. Shurden says that when Holcomb moved to Nashville in 1935, he hung a picture of a small rural church in his office. It symbolized his dream for the next eighteen years—an all-out effort to assist the least church in the most remote area.

Holcomb's appreciation for the ministry of music is illustrated in what happened in Oklahoma City, where he was pastor of the First Baptist

Church during the Great Depression. Suicides were common throughout
the city. Luther Holcomb, his son, tells what his Dad did:

> One day my father took me along with him to see the city man-
> ager. As soon as he saw my father in the reception room he said,
> "Come on in, Preacher. You've come down here to talk about sui-
> cides, and there is nothing I can do about them." My father told
> him that he wanted permission to go on the streets of Oklahoma
> City after the Sunday evening services. "I don't want to preach. I
> want a truck, and I want a choir, and I want that choir to sing
> hymns like 'How Firm a Foundation,' 'Blessed Assurance,' and
> 'Amazing Grace.' All I want to do is stand up on the back of that
> truck and read verses such as 'God is our refuge and strength, a
> very present help in trouble.'"

The city manager approved, and the choir from the downtown First Baptist Church was soon singing from a truckbed.

In his own words, T. L. Holcomb told how he interviewed McKinney for
the job. In a September 12, 1952 memorial service for McKinney held at the
Sunday School Board in Nashville, Holcomb explained:

> I went out to Ft. Worth many years ago to see if he would come
> with us. I talked with him all morning. It was awful: I did not
> know what to tell him; I did not know what to say. Finally, noon
> came and I don't suppose he quite knew how to get rid of me. So I
> just went home with him. Mrs. McKinney had a good lunch and
> we talked and visited. We talked about Sunday School and Train-
> ing Union, and everything, and I still had not told him why I had
> come. I was almost ready to come back to Nashville, so as we
> went to the train, I said, "I have come out here to ask you some-
> thing." And out of that conversation we have had the marvelous
> service of Dr. McKinney.

McKinney accepted Holcomb's offer and on December 1, 1935, joined
the staff of the Board as music editor.

It was a hard blow to Travis Avenue Baptist Church. Writing in the October 4, 1935 Travis Avenue edition of the *Ft. Worth Tribune*, pastor C. E. Mat-

thews said: "Our hearts are saddened and shocked at losing Brother and Mrs. McKinney . . . for there are no two people who can fill their places as song leader and B.T.U. director. We can only say, 'His will be done and not ours.' They move away from our church, but they will never be moved from our hearts. As pastor, I have worked seven years by the side of B. B. McKinney. In that seven years we have never had a cross word. If ever two men had a kindred spirit, I believe we have."

And in the November 29, 1935 issue of the same paper, Matthews urged all members to be present the following Sunday night for an appreciation service. He pointed out that during the years McKinney was on the staff, he served as associate pastor as well as music director. He also mentioned that during this time, their two sons, B. B., Jr. and Gene, had been baptized.

Four years later, in 1939, deacon W. B. McClure wrote to Mrs. McKinney that "Travis Avenue is still prospering (but) the church felt a dull thud when the undergirding of the McKinneys slipped out from under the load."

At least two times, Travis Avenue attempted to call the McKinneys back to Fort Worth from Nashville. On January 25, 1939, Matthews wrote them:

> I am writing this after one year's meditation, prayer and the very best thinking I am capable of doing. Our church never had and never will have two people so universally in their hearts (big, little, old, and young) as the McKinneys are. If you will come back, we will give you a unanimous call. B. B. can have his connection with Coleman. And Mrs. Mac, you can be educational director, Sunday School and all if you want it. I will covenant to stay with you until the Lord calls me home.

Then on May 26, 1945, Matthews wrote again:

> Somehow I am convinced that it is the will of God for you two to give the rest of your lives here. I do not know why I feel that way. I believe you would be happier and that your work would be much more profitable.

Matthews apparently received a telegram refusing the latest offer, for on May 29, 1945, he replied:

Of course I would have loved to have had you folks back here for the rest of your days and I believe 100% of the members would feel the same way. But God's will be done, not ours. I do not know what the Seminary is going to do about their department of music. I think I told you that I have been elected president of the Board. Dr. Head is very prayerfully considering the matter of music . . . It is a very difficult situation, but God has somebody for that place. One thing I know . . . from here on in Travis Avenue . . . we are going to have simple, plain gospel music."

The die was cast. B. B. McKinney would never again serve on a church staff.

First published in the May 1950 issue of *Home Life* magazine and introduced at the 1950 Southern Baptist Convention in Chicago by the Bison Glee Club, this number reflects his years with the Baptist Sunday School Board:

God, Give Us Christian Homes

1. God, give us Chris-tian homes! Homes where the Bi-ble is loved and taught, Homes where the Mas-ter's will is sought, Homes crowned with beau-ty thy love hath wrought; God, give us Chris-tian homes; God, give us Chris-tian homes!
2. God, give us Chris-tian homes! Homes where the fa-ther is true and strong, Homes that are free from the blight of wrong, Homes that are joy-ous with love and song; God, give us Chris-tian homes; God, give us Chris-tian homes!
3. God, give us Chris-tian homes! Homes where the moth-er, in queen-ly quest, Strives to show oth-ers thy way is best, Homes where the Lord is an hon-ored guest; God, give us Chris-tian homes; God, give us Chris-tian homes!
4. God, give us Chris-tian homes! Homes where the chil-dren are led to know Christ in his beau-ty who loves them so, Homes where the al-tar fires burn and glow; God, give us Chris-tian homes; God, give us Chris-tian homes! A - MEN.

4
"We Were Feeling Our Way"

"Hooraw and another hooraw" is how music professor E. O. Sellers of New Orleans Baptist Seminary began a letter of congratulations to B. B. McKinney on his new job as music editor at the Baptist Sunday School Board. "At last Southern Baptists have taken an advance step in regards to their music."

"Brother Beloved" is how J. L. Blankenship of Puente, California began his letter. "We predict that what Dr. Frost was to the Sunday School Board and the Leavell brothers to Baptist Training Unions, you will be to the no less opportunity of church music."

"You have come to the Kingdom at a time to render a great service," is how Bernard W. Spilman of Kinston, North Carolina wrote him after he'd been on the job a few months.

"Dear Big Ben" is the way Lemuel J. Hall of Granite City, Illinois began his October 9, 1935 letter of congratulation. And from Nashville, Andrew Allen wrote, "You and Mrs. McKinney won't like Nashville at first because of the smoke, and coming here at that time of the year you will find it at its worst."

Although B. B. began work December 1, 1935, Mrs. McKinney and their teenage boys, Gene, thirteen, and B. B., Jr., fifteen, stayed in Fort Worth until after the holidays. The three of them, plus their dog, arrived by car at 10:30 on a Friday night in mid-January, in zero weather. The next day, Saturday, they moved into a house at 1605 Cedar Lane. It would be McKinney's last home—he lived here until his death seventeen years later. Mrs. McKinney lived here nearly forty-eight years, until 1983.

The following Sunday, the McKinneys joined the First Baptist Church in Nashville. Two weeks later, Mrs. McKinney began teaching a Sunday School class and he served as a deacon.

McKinney, now forty-nine years of age, found no ruts cut out for him at the Board. There was no tradition of church music promoted on a national basis. He was the program, and the program was he—that is, whatever he could make of it.

The following spring, the Board's report to the 1936 Southern Baptist Convention noted that McKinney "will help to produce and promote through our periodicals the right kind of music for our churches. As Music Leader in training schools, assemblies, and conventions he will be the exponent and advocate of music that will be sound in its melody and spiritual in its impress."

But throughout his Nashville career, McKinney continued his peripatetic role as "Mr. Music Ambassador-at-Large." He had full privileges to accept personal invitations for revivals and conferences, and for this reason came to the Board at less than full salary. This was in effect until his death in 1952.

When he reported for work that December morning in 1935, he made the fifth "general" editor on the staff of the Board. The other four were editorial secretary Hight C Moore, his associate John C. Slemp, managing editor Noble Van Ness, and art editor Herman F. Burns. Although a major publisher of all kinds of church materials, the Board in 1935 had only thirteen other editors, including book editor John L. Hill of Broadman Press.

For example, during those Depression years, J. E. Lambdin, secretary of the Training Union department, edited one monthly and six quarterly publications himself!

T. L. Holcomb, the Board's executive secretary, said he put McKinney under Hight C Moore so he could "feel at ease" and have "an opportunity to get acclimated into the whole field . . . we were feeling our way (at the time)." Once McKinney started editing hymnals, there was a working relationship with Hill of Broadman Press.

Within two years (in 1937) McKinney had his first hymnbook edited and ready for sale. It was a paperback of 109 hymns titled *Songs of Victory*. William J. Reynolds, one of McKinney's biographers, says this collection marked the first publication of his two best gospel songs, "Wherever He Leads I'll Go" and "Holy Spirit, Breathe on Me."

Another paperback, The *Song Evangel*, appeared in 1940, the year that also saw the publication of *The Broadman Hymnal*.

William Reynolds relates a story about *Songs of Victory* which his uncle, Isham Reynolds, told him. "I have no other validation of this information," he said. The story is that in the early months of his employment in Nashville, B. B. started work on a large hymnal. When it was completed, he showed the "dummy" layout to John L. Hill. Although Hill was aware of Holcomb's support of McKinney, he felt the new compilation was below the quality he desired. Yet he didn't feel he could cancel the project because of Holcomb's backing. So he asked B. B. to cut the number of pages because of the costs of paper and printing. After several such requests, B. B. cut it to about ninety-seven pages, which was then published in paperback.

An immediate problem facing McKinney was the question of copyrights. Prior to 1937, the Hope Publishing Company had produced the songbooks sold by the Baptist Sunday School Board. This company owned the copyrights to most of the best-known and best-loved hymns of Southern Baptists. And Robert Coleman owned copyrights for much of McKinney's work.

The first move was to secure the copyrights owned by Coleman. T. L. Holcomb told how it happened in an interview during a September 21, 1965 visit to Nashville:

> I wrote Mr. Coleman asking if he would be interested in selling his entire music business—books and his copyrights and all of it and his good will. He wrote back that he would be interested but that he first must find out if any member of his family wanted to carry on. . . . I thought that was fine of him toward his family and so he wrote me in a few days and said that neither one of the grandsons felt inclined to giving their life to that type of thing. And he said, "I am willing to sell."
>
> I wrote back immediately and asked him to make a price. He was not well and I knew it and there was not time to argue with the man when he had the thing we needed both in the matter of publicity and in the matter of copyright. It's the first time I ever made a trade without asking, "Can't you do a little better?" I never asked him because I felt that too much was involved for Southern Baptists for me to get in an argument about a few dol-

lars. I just wrote him that we would be glad to accept his terms
and for him to have the papers prepared.

The Board paid Coleman $50,000 for his business, including what copy-
rights he owned, payable in installments. John Williams of the Board staff
went to Dallas to inventory the business. Holcomb added:

> When Coleman died, we asked the family if they would like for
> us to pay it all in cash. They said no, they wanted it carried out
> just as he had arranged. As I remember, it guaranteed him that
> his immediate family—grandchildren and all of that—would have
> a rather substantial income for a number of years. I yielded to his
> will in the whole thing because he had put his life into it and loved
> it. (Until that time) I don't think we (the Board) had any copy-
> rights at all.

The next step was to secure permissions from the Hope Publishing
Company. This was not easy. James L. Sullivan, Holcomb's successor at
the Board, tells the story. McKinney told him the details when the two
were in a revival in 1950 in West Tennessee:

> To produce a quality hymnal would require many more hymns
> and gospel songs than the Board owned. But when McKinney
> approached Hope Publishing, they were hesitant to let him have
> any of their copyrights. Finally, after urging, they agreed to let
> him have a certain number on a financially progressive basis.
> That is, they would charge $25 for the first hymn, $50 for the sec-
> ond, $100 for the third, $200 for the fourth, etc.
> Still, they limited the number (of hymns) even with that finan-
> cially impossible arrangement. On top of that, they said, "We will
> not sell you the right to use 'Power in the Blood' at any cost."
> Having secured all the copyrights economically feasible, he
> produced *The Broadman Hymnal* and it was highly successful,
> with a massive acceptance by Southern Baptists. Its success
> brought McKinney some real grief. Being artistic by nature, he
> was very sensitive to criticism. This is where Hope hit him hard.

Hope Publishing evidently was the one that spread widely that the reason 'Power in the Blood' was not in *The Broadman Hymnal* was that McKinney and Southern Baptists no longer believed in the substitutionary atonement of Jesus and therefore left it out on purpose—although they knew full well they had refused the copyright at any price.

McKinney was wounded in soul and literally wept tears as he spoke of such injustice, after he had given his life to singing and writing about the crucifixion.

Perhaps this explains why these privately owned publishers never used McKinney's songs very much. They were afraid others would be drawn to his publications.

On this same subject, Walter W. Jacobs of Greenville, South Carolina wrote me, "It would be interesting to your readers to give them background on *The Broadman Hymnal* and why it included such numbers as *The Hallelujah Chorus* (not singable by most Baptist congregations) and other 'filler.' It was because we owned no copyrights and consequently couldn't swap for songs we wanted and couldn't afford to buy them."

Following McKinney's death, Holcomb told in a chapel service at the Board about a "great song leader" who once came for a conference and said, "We've had so much of that about the blood, let's sing the inspirational songs that will make men want to live." Later, McKinney told Holcomb, "A man isn't ready to live until he has had the cleansing of the blood of the Lord Jesus Christ."

Dr. Sullivan told me how the rumor was finally squelched. He learned about it after he became executive-secretary of the Board. At the time, all typesetting for music was done by hand. And there was only one typesetter in the business that set type for hymnals—The Andersen Typesetting Company in Chicago.

Leaders at the Board knew Mr. Andersen was getting old and might be interested in selling. When the Board made him an offer, he took it and the company was moved to Nashville.

Next, the Board notified Hope Publishing Company that from here on, type would be set for them only when they were willing to sell copyrights to Broadman.

"This seemed to be the only language Hope could understand," Sullivan told me. "Too, with the Board's advantage, the rumors about McKinney and the Board's not believing in the cross of Christ stopped immediately. While I haven't seen firm statements saying so, I know enough about the Board's mode of operation to conclude that McKinney was in on this action to silence the rumor and get needed copyrights also."

In spite of such limitations, McKinney's *The Broadman Hymnal* "probably experienced a distribution of more copies than any other hymnal published in this century," according to William J. Reynolds. "It did more to unify Southern Baptist music than any hymnal. It was our first time to have a common hymnal. Before, you could cross a county line to lead music in a revival, and find they were using an entirely different book."

Walter B. Shurden pays tribute to *The Broadman Hymnal* in his 1981 history of the Sunday School Board. He said that other than the Bible, this hymnal was Southern Baptists' only "Book of Common Prayer."

It was seven years, however, before McKinney wrote promotional materials, on a regular basis, to assist churches in their music programs. That started with the January 1942 issue of *Training Union Magazine*. For five years, through December of 1947, he wrote a monthly column, "Let us Sing," in the magazine. The idea probably originated with Wayne R. Maddox, a teenager from Appalachia, Virginia, who met him at Ridgecrest one summer and expressed a desire for written helps on a regular basis.

Beginning in the January 1948 issue, W. Hines Sims wrote a column under a new title, "Musical Notes."

1942 also saw the publication of *Let Us Sing*, one of the first church music study course books published by any denomination. It was co-authored by McKinney and Allen W. Graves, later a professor at Southern Baptist Seminary in Louisville, Kentucky.

Graves, a staff member at the Board in 1941-43, wrote chapters 1, 2, and 5. "I was more interested in worshipful music, while McKinney insisted on gospel songs and choruses," Graves told me. "We competed over who would have the last say about the contents—but it was all done in good humor. Actually, McKinney knew little about writing. I think that's why they got me to help."

Looking back on those years, Graves added, "McKinney wasn't an administrator. I doubt if he knew what direction the music program would take. He wouldn't see himself in that role today. Even then, he preferred being out in revivals and conventions, not in the office."

Actually, four authors had a part in the book, for Robbie Trent wrote chapter 4 for music leaders with youth ages nine to sixteen. Mattie C. Leatherwood produced chapter 3 for workers with younger children. McKinney wrote chapters 6, 7, 8, and 9.

Browsing through the book, one is impressed with its practical approach. For example, take chapter 6, "Let All the People Sing." McKinney divides the chapter into six topics—let the people sing with volume, let them sing beautifully, let them sing worshipfully, let them sing great hymns, let them sing gospel hymns, and let them sing new hymns.

Apparently drawing on his years at Travis Avenue Church, he advised:

> Some choir members prefer to sit only on the front row. A good plan is to change the seating of the choir every six months. The director would do well to advise every singer that possession for a length of time gives no title to a certain seat; that no member of any choir is to "own" any seat, but that each will be seated according to the plan of the director.

On page 106, he defines gospel music:

> What is the difference between the gospel hymn and the standard hymn? . . . . as a rule, the standard hymn is more scriptural in sentiment, more stately and devotional in character, more refined in poetic language, more excellent in literary and musical quality, and more varied in harmonic and melodic structure. It seldom has a chorus.
>
> The gospel hymn is more informal, more evangelistic in its appeal, more singable as a rule, more simplified in melody and harmony, more rhythmical, more emotional, and more adaptable to mass singing. It usually has a chorus.

This book also dealt with graded choirs. Age-group, robed choirs are so common today that we take them for granted. It was not always so.

This is another topic T. L. Holcomb discussed in his far-ranging September 21, 1965 interview cited earlier. Holcomb credits himself with introducing the idea of graded choirs at the Board and some of the initial publicity in *The Sunday School Builder* magazine.

In the summer of 1936, Holcomb supplied the pulpit at the First Baptist Church in Bessemer, Alabama. There—apparently for the first time—he saw an aggressive graded choir program. He liked it and came back to Nashville, promoting such.

For one thing, he liked the attractive robes the children wore. He felt this added to a worshipful spirit, in that every singer was dressed alike. "I counted right there in the First Baptist Church seventeen different types of hat the women had on," he reported. "Now that wasn't conducive to worship or even listening to the preacher. It was more like a style show and they were all fitted up, too, in pretty good hats."

In the interview, Holcomb continued:

> I went into the church that morning and they had graded choirs in uniforms (robes). I knew right then that there was too much good looks about that group of young people and that that thing was going to spread. I came back and told Harold Ingraham about it and so he published it in *The Builder*. I knew just as well as I knew the ABC's that this thing of graded choirs—Junior, Intermediate, etc.—was going to take.
>
> Mr. Ingraham asked me, "Do you feel safe to publish (photos of) choirs with robes on?" I said I know I feel safer than I do to let it go by without doing anything about it. So we went ahead with it.

Apparently, McKinney "went ahead with it" too!

In my research, I ran across a delightful letter from a boy in another Alabama church who later benefited from graded choirs. It's in boyish handwriting from Steve Taylor to McKinney's widow on June 27, 1962. Steve lived in Mobile, Alabama, where he attended the Cottage Hill Baptist Church, Ernest S. Owens, pastor.

Here is Steve's letter, with his exact spelling, punctuation, and line length:

> Mrs. McKinney
> I go to Cottage Hill churnk.

I go to Chair. I have been
Singin songs that your Husband Wrote
I am in Pairmars II. My name is
Steve T.   I like the song that your
Husband wrote. Mrs. Albritton
went Ridgecrest.
This month we have
been studay about b. b. M.
I hope you don't get lonesome
when you saty home.
I will tell you about my Father's
work. My Father works for the
Internal Revenue.

Good-by,
by Steve Taylor.

At least Steve knew how to spell his Dad's job! Who knows, Steve may be a big wheel in the IRS today!

As interest grew in the churches, the monthly music columns in the *Training Union Magazine* were not enough. So on October 1, 1950, a new monthly, *The Church Musician,* came off the presses. Initial circulation was 18,000 copies. W. Hines Sims, now a staff member too, served as editor with McKinney as music editor. It contained thirty-six pages, including sixteen pages of choir music.

The anthems in each issue were also marketed as separate choral octavos by Broadman Press. William J. Reynolds notes that whereas McKinney often joked about church choirs who sang anthems, he was the one who initiated anthem publishing by the Board!

But we're getting ahead of our story, at least chronologically. Let's go back to 1941, the year church music was established as a department at the Board.

Sentiment continued to grow for the Board to do more than publish helps under the direction of a music editor. Isham E. Reynolds of Southwestern Seminary seems to have been most relentless in pressing the denomination to do more.

Reynolds was one of five prominent persons who offered a resolution to the Southern Baptist Convention meeting in New Orleans in 1937. The resolution, also signed by Inman Johnson of Louisville, E. O. Sellers of New Orleans, J. W. Storer of Tulsa, and B. B. McKinney of Nashville, asked for a committee "to make a study of the present conditions and needs affecting our Church Music." The committee was appointed and, among other things, made a survey of Southern Baptist churches which showed that gospel songs were preferred by 68 percent of those responding. It also revealed that more churches picked McKinney's songs as favorites than any other composer.

On August 20, 1941, the executive committee of the Board approved a new Department of Church Music. A mail poll of other members of the Board was unanimously in favor. McKinney was immediately promoted from music editor to secretary of the new department.

McKinney's tenous relationship with Isham E. Reynolds surfaced again during his years in Nashville. On April 18, 1936, McKinney wrote to Reynolds at Seminary Hill, Texas:

> Because of reasons well known by all those who attended the Music Conference at Mineral Wells, I feel that it would be best for us not to appear on the same conference program again. There should be harmony and fellowship in all the meetings.
>
> Therefore I must decline the invitation to appear on your program next fall. We have and are publishing much literature for the rural people.

Apparently McKinney and Reynolds had disagreed publicly at some meeting. McKinney felt strongly the two shouldn't appear again on the same platform.

From the tone of Reynolds' two-page, single-spaced reply on May 5, 1936, the disagreement was over special helps—or maybe a hymnal—for rural churches. Reynolds felt there was no need to publish materials aimed, say, at churches with limited leadership. Rather, he felt churches could choose for themselves what they felt was helpful. In part, Reynolds wrote back:

> Am very sorry you feel you cannot attend our Southwest Church Music Conference here this winter.

I was surprised beyond measure at your reference to the lack of harmony and fellowship in the Conference at Mineral Wells. There was nothing personal in anything I had to say.

You cannot expect to hold conferences anywhere and have everybody agree with you. Growth does not come that way. It comes through the consideration and exchange of different ideas.

Now as to rural problems, as stated at Mineral Wells, the Board promotes a high standard of literature for the Southern Baptist constituency. This literature is sent to city and country alike, without distinction between the places to which it is sent. It is expected of those who teach it that they should know how to present it to the people. Just so should it be with the music.

I am sure there is a place for the theory book, which you mentioned, and it can be used to splendid advantage not only in the rural districts but in the city as well. . . . the fact that our ideas run contrary to each other is no reason why we should not be any the less friends and co-workers.

From my research, I'm certain that McKinney changed his mind and did attend Reynolds' conference that winter. But when I started to write, I could not locate or document this.

In an unpublished manuscript in the B. B. McKinney collection at the Dargan Research Library in Nashville, I found where McKinney said one goal of his department was: "To offer all assistance possible to the neglected, misguided rural churches, many of which have been misled by commercialized leaders of cheap, undesirable music." This is an apparent reference to "foot-music," which he disdained.

Likewise, he had little time for "professional" church music. In another unpublished manuscript, he describes a church where two professional musicians—a soprano and a tenor—sang solos. "He impressed, but he did not inspire," McKinney concluded.

McKinney was the only staff member of the Church Music Department for the first five years. Then in 1946 Walter Hines Sims was named his associate. And 1951 saw the employment of a third staffer—Alta C. Faircloth, whose father McKinney had known at Southwestern Seminary. She had editing responsibilities. At first, the three of them, with no separate offices, worked in one room with only partitions between their desks.

In 1946 the Board encouraged music leadership in the various states by offering to pay one-third of the salary of any well-qualified, full-time state music secretary. The first five states to accept the offer were Texas, Arkansas, Mississippi, Oklahoma, and Florida.

According to Holcomb's September 21, 1965 interview, the first to accept the offer was Arkansas "and the funny thing about it was they got a woman." She was Mrs. Ruth Nininger, who also pioneered in state festivals for graded choirs, an idea that spread quickly to other states.

In January of 1946, McKinney convened the first meeting of those five state directors—J. D. Riddle, Ruth Nininger, Luther Harrison, Ira C. Prosser, and C. A. Holcomb.

These Nashville meetings of state music secretaries continued each December. Eugene F. Quinn of Louisville, Kentucky remembers going to his first one, in December of 1947, as Illinois music secretary. He recalls McKinney, Sims, Faircloth, and the five persons mentioned above as being present. "We had warm fellowship and cordial discussions about what direction the work should go as we met around that table each December in the old Frost Building until McKinney's death in 1952," he said.

We cannot close McKinney's work at the Sunday School Board until we look at what he did at Ridgecrest Baptist Conference Center in North Carolina.

The first "official" Church Music Week at Ridgecrest was in 1949. Paul R. Powell's research led him to believe that the first "Southwide Church Music Emphasis Conference" was in the summer of 1940, co-sponsored by the Sunday School Board and the Home Mission Board.

However, Warren M. Angell of Shawnee, Oklahoma told me the first emphasis was during the summer of 1938. Angell says he should know "because I was there, a member of the faculty, and I was only 30 at the time" (Angell was born in 1907).

Angell, the dean of the College of Fine Arts at Oklahoma Baptist University, recalls an attendance of a mere fourteen persons with E. O. Sellers and Isham Reynolds on the faculty too.

"Reynolds and Sellers made light of it to McKinney's back," Angell said. "McKinney then told me that next year, he'd have the biggest crowd you ever saw, not just fourteen. Back then, no one had money to go all the way to North Carolina to a music event. The next year he got the Sunday School Board to help with travel expenses, and a crowd showed up, just like he'd said. However, most of them came from North Carolina."

Angell recalls that during the summer of 1939, the Oratorio Choir got so large it moved to the main auditorium for its presentations. "We built up to 500 in the choir," he told me. "Stage wouldn't hold everyone—put some in seats down in front. We did lots of oratorios—St. Matthew Passion, The Messiah, and Elijah."

Eugene F. Quinn, at the time from Illinois, remembers 1941 as his first year at a music conference at Ridgecrest:

> I met Dr. McKinney for the first time that summer. I sang in *The Messiah* when practically the whole conference was in the Oratorio Choir. The congregation consisted of local people as well as (summer) staff members.

Mrs. John E. (Louise) Farmer of Cayce, South Carolina has fond memories of McKinney, ringing a handbell, coming down the hill by the auditorium, announcing the start of another class or time of inspiration.

William J. Reynolds' first music week at Ridgecrest was the summer of 1948. He remembers it in connection with other conferences, such as church library, church architecture, and church history. About three hundred musicians were present, and their classes disturbed some of the other sessions. They said the singers should go "off down the road somewhere by themselves."

After McKinney shared his dreams of a week exclusively for music, William J. Reynolds made a motion for such on the last day of the assembly. McKinney took the request back to Nashville, and soon T. L. Holcomb announced that he'd found a niche on the 1949 calendar for a Church Music Week just for music.

Such persons as Warren Angell, E. O. Sellers, I. E. Reynolds, Inman

Johnson, and Claude Almand returned summer after summer as faculty members.

Each year attendance grew rapidly. McKinney's final dream came true. And strangely, his last public appearance was at Ridgecrest in August of 1952.

But first, a look at more aspects of his Nashville years.

James Calvin and Martha McKinney with 9 of their 11 children, 1899. B. B., far right, hair parted in middle, was 13. Another son, James B., had died in 1880. Still another son, Lawson Bryant, was born in the following year, 1900.

Leila Routh McKinney, age 15, shortly before she entered college.

Floor plan of B. B.'s boyhood home in Heflin, Louisiana: a double-pen, split-log house built by James Calvin McKinney about 1875. The two large bedrooms/sitting rooms were about twenty feet square. Winborn Davis contributed the floor plan.

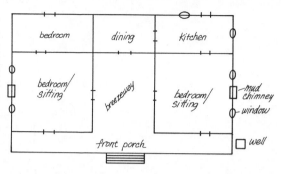

bedroom | dining | kitchen

bedroom/ sitting | breezeway | bedroom/ sitting

—mud chimney

—window

front porch

□ well

Boyhood home in 1958, not long before it was torn down. Tin roof was not original.

The Bistineau Baptist Church near Heflin, Louisiana, as it looked when B. B. was a boy. This building was erected in 1872 and was used for worship until about 1936.

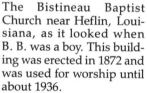

The restored McKinney family organ, around which the family sang. Gloria Smith Moore of Coushatta, Louisiana, who restored it, left a scorched spot which resulted from the many years a kerosene lamp sat on it.

The McKinneys, shortly after their marriage in 1918.

McKinney in World War I uniform, 1918.

McKinney as student or young professor, Southwestern Baptist Theological Seminary, about 1918.

McKinney and E. L. Carnett, Southwestern Seminary, 1920s.

McKinney and Isham Reynolds in front of Fort Worth Hall, Southwestern Seminary, late 1920s.

McKinney, top, in male quartet at Southwestern Seminary, 1919-1921. Others are, from left, Theodore H. Farr, a Mr. Stultz, and a Mr. Odom.

The McKinney sons, Eugene and
B. B., Jr., about 1932.

B. B. McKinney and son, Baylus,
Jr., downtown Nashville, late
1930s.

Joanna McKinney Smith, B. B.'s
oldest sister, whom he called his
"Mama" after their mother died.
Joanna hosted the annual reunions until her death in 1967.

Top—McKinney, Fort Worth, early 1930s.

Left—McKinney, probably on vacation to Louisiana in late 1920s.

Right—McKinney with evangelist Hyman Appleman and pastor C. E. Matthews on steps of Travis Avenue Baptist Church, Fort Worth, early 1930s.

The McKinney home at 4504 Frazier on Seminary Hill, as it looked when they lived there the years he served Southwestern Seminary and Travis Avenue Baptist Church.

The home at 4504 Frazier as it looked in 1983 when used as a visual during the production of "A Different Drummer" at the seminary.

McKinney with Mr. and Mrs.
E. E. Lee in front of the "Hot Dog
Hut" he shared with them at Falls
Creek.

Training Union group at First Baptist Church, Nashville, late 1930s, when
Mrs. McKinney was director.

McKinney dominated the center of this group photo of his music class at Falls Creek, summer of 1937.

An outdoor social event during World War II involving young people from First Baptist Church, Nashville, with Mrs. McKinney as director.

Left—The McKinneys in front of First Baptist Church, Nashville, about 1940.

Below—McKinney, right, looks on while Porter W. Routh and T. L. Holcomb read a telegram from Billy Graham at the start of his Boston crusade about 1945. Graham was asking permission to use McKinney's song "Lord, Send a Revival" as a theme for his crusades. It was so used for several years.

Bottom—Porter W. Routh and his family, left, join Dr. and Mrs. McKinney in a family sing in Nashville in the 1940s. This is not the organ from B. B.'s boyhood home, but one he later purchased.

McKinney, a portrait.

The McKinneys at
Ridgecrest, about 1946.

McKinney, left, with War-
ren Angell and W. Hines
Sims, Ridgecrest, late
1940s.

McKinney, seated second from right, with 1944 music faculty at Ridgecrest.

World War II photos of the McKinney sons, Eugene and B. B., Jr.

McKinney with seven of his brothers and sisters, about 1950. The brothers, from left, are Kieffer, Hildebrand, B. B., Thomas, and Will. The sisters, from left, are Carrie McKinney Smith, Litha McKinney Tyler, and Joanna McKinney Davis. All are deceased.

The McKinneys, Ridgecrest, August 1952. This picture was taken the same day as the picture below.

McKinney with Mrs. McKinney and T. L. Holcomb, Ridgecrest, August 1952. This picture and the one at left are the last two photos taken of McKinney before his death.

McKinney, about 1951.

McKinney's desk as he left it before going to Ridgecrest, August 1952. Leila's photo sits on desk. Sallman's "Head of Christ" is at the top of the wall display. Below it is his honorary doctorate from Oklahoma Baptist University. The next three photos are Robert Coleman, George W. Truett, and Hight C Moore. The next three are son Eugene, B. W. Spilman, and son B. B., Jr. (in uniform of the Cowboy Band at Hardin-Simmons University). The plaque at the bottom reads, "Prayer Changes Things."

Mrs. McKinney with Gene Bartlett at 1965 dedication of B. B. McKinney Chapel at Falls Creek.

Leila McKinney, the photo released by Baptist Press at her death in 1985.

Mrs. McKinney at dedication of marker at Falls Creek in 1978.

Mrs. McKinney recognized at PraiSing 75, Nashville, as part of the tribute to B. B. McKinney. She is flanked by McKinney's successors at the Sunday School Board, William J. Reynolds (left) and W. Hines Sims (right).

Mrs. McKinney recognized in 1982 at the Dove Awards Presentation, Nashville, when B. B. McKinney was inducted into the Gospel Music Hall of Fame. Don Butler, executive director of the Gospel Music Association, is at right; Wesley L. Forbis, director of the Sunday School Board's Church Music Department, is at left (photo by Bill Preston).

I SHALL NOT LIVE IN VAIN

B. B. McKinney

If I can plant a rose where thorns have been,
Dispel the gloom, and let the sunshine in;
If I can help some broken life to rise again,
  I shall not live in vain.

If I can sing a song of love and cheer,
Some song that lifts a soul from doubt and fear,
And bring them back to know that God is always near,
  I shall not live in vain.

If I can be a light wher-e'er I go,
A light to shine for those in sin and woe,
If I can lead some soul my living Christ to know,
  I shall not live in vain.

McKinney once told his brother-in-law, E. C. Routh, that the most moving experience of his life was when he heard "a group of 30 or 40 ragged, Mexican orphans" sing this number:

He Lives On High

Words by
B. B. McKinney

Arr. by B. B. McKinney
From Hawaiian Folk Song

1. Christ the Sav - iour came from heaven's glo - ry, To re - deem the lost from sin and shame; On His brow He wore the thorn-crown go - ry, And up - on Cal - va - ry He took my blame.

2. He a - rose from death and all its sor - row, To dwell in that land of joy and love; He is com - ing back some glad to - mor - row, And He'll take all His chil - dren home a - bove.

3. Wea - ry soul, to Je - sus come con - fess - ing, Re - demp-tion from sin He of - fers thee; Look to Je - sus and re - ceive a bless - ing, There is life, there is joy and vic - to - ry.

CHORUS

He lives on high, He lives on high, Tri-um-phant o - ver sin and all its stain; He lives on high, He lives on high, Some day He's com-ing a - gain.

5
"He Lifted Me Over the Gate"

To know the real B. B. McKinney, you must look beyond his role as an editor and denominational official and listen to those who knew him. So I've chosen to devote one entire chapter to a sampling of letters I received in 1983-84. Most of these testimonies relate to his Nashville years.

John S. Burton of Long Beach, California prizes a hand-written copy of a poem, "Dear Old Dad," which McKinney wrote for his use on Father's Day. It was during a revival in the 1930s when Burton was music director at First Southern Baptist Church in Phoenix, Arizona. McKinney wrote it on the back of the Sunday School Board stationery. The first verse goes like this:

> When you praise your precious Mother
> For her love and godly life,
> For her counsel and protection
> Thru the storm and thru the strife,
> Just remember there's another
> Who is often lone and sad.
> So when'er you praise your Mother,
> Don't forget your dear old Dad.

Irene Pickering prizes his autograph he gave her in 1942 at Ridgecrest. It's a variation of one cited earlier in this book:

Fay H. Humphrey of Maryville, Tennessee remembers when McKinney played a guitar to accompany himself in a revival in the 1940s, "an unheard of event in our church!" And in the same service, Mrs. McKinney "played" ordinary water glasses in a beautiful manner (i.e., striking glasses filled with varying levels of water, to achieve a melody). And Mrs. J. S. Holmes wrote him in 1935 from Abilene, Texas to report that her two sons, Jentry and Paul, ages twelve and fourteen, felt "the radio programs seem tame after hearing Bro. McKinney."

Miss Ferris Carper of Dallas once rode to church with McKinney in a wagon, when the roads were too muddy for a car. She was eight at the time: "I still remember how he picked me up and lifted me out of the wagon, over the front gate." And Nellie Kerby of Cushing, Oklahoma, who describes herself as "a real Baptist," recalls that "everyone nearly sang their hearts out" when McKinney led a revival in Guthrie, Oklahoma years ago.

Mrs. Walton (Sue) Conn of Nashville, Tennessee grew up in a pastor's home in South Carolina where McKinney visited frequently. She recalls:

> My father, the late Eugene R. Eller, provided the best for his members. He planned years ahead to invite outstanding men to our church, much to the amazement of many of his fellow pastors. Thus, B. B. McKinney became a friend of our family.
>
> One afternoon Mother came home to find Dr. McKinney on his all-fours, riding my 4-year-old brother around the living room on his back. And he would rearrange our porch furniture into a train and play choo-choo with my brother and me. The sound effects he provided were magnificent as we took turns sitting on his lap and playing conductor, engineer, or passenger.
>
> When he came for a revival in the First Baptist Church, Pickens, I was one of the accompanists. I was a teenager and the thought of accompanying a famous composer unnerved me completely. He did all he could—almost—to put me at ease. However, he never gave me a complete order of service. If he gave me one at all, he changed it as he got the "feel" of that particular service.
>
> During one service, a 4-year-old girl stood up on the pew be-

tween her parents and cried so all could hear, "Sing, Kinney, sing!" And in another revival at Pickens, he wrote the chorus, *My All for Jesus,* at our kitchen table and dedicated it to the B. B. McKinney Youth Choir of our church.

Donald I. Moore of Waco, Texas remembers being in the balcony at Ridgecrest, waiting for an evening service to begin, when McKinney came on stage to set up some chairs. Donald Moore turned to Mrs. McKinney nearby and said, "Younger people should be doing that kind of work." She replied, "There's no job too small for him if it's the Lord's work."

Ben R. Stripling of Tyler, Texas says that when members hosted McKinney for meals during a revival, he'd say to the hostess, "I'm sorry, Ma'am, but I'm on an eight-inch diet." And she'd reply, "Oh, I'm sorry, Dr. McKinney, what kind of diet is that?" Then he'd explain, "When I sit down, I place my chair eight inches from the table and when I eat up to it, I stop!"

William N. McElrath of Bandung, Indonesia, can never forget the time McKinney and J. O. Williams had breakfast at his home when they were in Murray, Kentucky for a revival. Bill, a little boy at the time, remembers how friendly Dr. McKinney was to him. He wrote in their guestbook:

Always B#
Never Bb
Keep all
your troubles
under your

W. H. Donaldson, black retired pastor in Champaign, Illinois, remembers when he and his wife, Clara, were students at the American Baptist Theological Seminary in Nashville about 1937. "Men from the Sunday School Board, such as T. L. Holcomb and E. P. Alldredge, often came out to lecture, and we liked them. B. B. McKinney came once. In chapel, he taught us one of his new hymns, "Wherever He leads I'll Go." When asked if any student would stand and sing it, Clara did. Then he gave her an autographed copy of *Songs of Victory* which he'd just published. I'll never forget him. He was so personable. He just beamed."

On April 28, 1949, Mrs. Franklin (Dorcas) Fowler, R.N., wrote him from the River Plate Baptist Mission in Asuncion, Paraguay:

> Many a night when I am alone at home with the children in bed and Franklin at church or elsewhere, I sit at the piano and go over and over many of my favorites which you have written. *Crowned or Crucified* never ceases to amaze and humble me.
>
> Being a missionary doesn't mean one is immune from being homesick and wanting the company of friends far away. But always when I feel that coming upon me, I have only to play or read your hymns and everything is alright again.

Franklin Fowler, M.D., penciled a P.S., "I can only add Amen."

Stories from Ridgecrest abound. Mrs. George (Evelyn) Fort of Nashville remembers when, at closing sessions, McKinney would pull out his white handkerchief and wave it as they sang, "God Be with You Till We Meet Again."

Mrs. R. E. (Ellen) Cauthen of Lancaster, South Carolina, was impressed at Ridgecrest when McKinney, night after night, led them in singing "I Love Him," with those on the main floor singing one phrase, those in the balcony singing the next one, like an echo. It still rings in her heart after forty years. And Wilmer C. Fields of Nashville, then a fifteen-year-old, recalls the day when McKinney chided the crowd for singing too slowly: "You folks sing like the L & NW Railroad down in Louisiana. The proper name is Louisiana and Northwest, but we called it Late and No Wonder." After the service, Wilmer introduced himself, saying he'd come to Ridgecrest on the L & NW on a pass, since his Dad was the railroad's agricultural agent. Wilmer also told him the latest nickname for the railroad: "Look North and Walk." McKinney put his arm around Wilmer's shoulder and had a big laugh.

M. G. Upton of Orangevale, California sent me this unique insight into McKinney at Ridgecrest:

It was during a Home Missions week. A youth evangelist and singer led one of the sessions. The invitation was a flimsy, every-body move, with "heads-bowed-and-eyes-closed" type. Every-one around me moved and I felt the pressure, but didn't feel I could respond in good faith.

It was then I dared sneak a peek. Only one other person was standing among the pews. It was McKinney, looking in my direc-tion. Something transpired in those glances between this stranger and me that was never mentioned. But through the years it has said to me, "He was my kind of man."

Robert E. Naylor, president emeritus of Southwestern Baptist Seminary, told me how McKinney led the singing in a revival at the First Baptist Church in Arkadelphia, Arkansas, where Naylor was pastor. He was stay-ing in their home. It was September of 1938, and the Naylors' oldest son was starting to school. "Mrs. Naylor loved having the children at home, and just permitting them to go off to school was one of those dreaded ne-cessities of growing up," Naylor said.

On the first day of school, the parents shined and polished the lad in his best and stood at the door, both of them crying, as he set off down the walk, carrying a new booksatchel. Then they heard a third person snif-fling. They turned and it was McKinney. "There we were, three grown people, crying over a six-year-old boy on his way to his first day of school," Naylor added. "Big as he was, McKinney grew in my estimation that morning."

Wesley L. Forbis of Nashville, one of McKinney's successors at the Sun-day School Board, described to me a revival in 1936 at the First Baptist Church in Chickasha, Oklahoma. "The winds of the Great Depression clouded our hopes as thoroughly as the dust filled our eyes," he said. "Pocketbooks were drawn as tightly as the dry lips which sought to close off the swirling grit. We were enclosed in an ever-tightening circle of misery—unaware of the spiritual and physical needs of those around us."

That year, Wesley recalls, the town was shocked when the church voted to build a large, outdoor tabernacle, the first of many projects of young pastor W. A. Criswell. Here, services could be held to escape the heat in-side the church. Also the 1936 summer revival was there:

Mother and I sat on the second row center. During the singing, I'd stand up on the pew and raise my six-year-old soprano voice with the others. The preacher, R. G. Lee, preached of a "payday." The singer, a genial giant by the name of B. B. McKinney, sang about "letting others see Jesus in you." Imagine my surprise when, after one service, he took me to the piano and taught me a new song. The next night, he called me to the rostrum, sat me on his knee and together we sang about being "Satisfied with Jesus."

When we finished, he scruffed my hair and said, "Now when you grow up, use your talent for the Lord."

Not until years later did the names of R. G. Lee and B. B. McKinney come to have significance. After 30 years of teaching, I became secretary of the Church Music Department at the Baptist Sunday School Board—a position first held by McKinney.

I begin each day reading from his pocket Bible (a gift of Mrs. McKinney) and humming those words learned so long ago, in 1936.

St. Louis pastor C. Oscar Johnson and McKinney were alike in that both were big men with humor and infectious smiles. The two men shared the program at a Tennessee State Evangelism Conference in Nashville's First Baptist Church.

While leading a song about prayer, McKinney stopped to tell about a boyhood illness when he was at the point of death. After describing how his mother knelt at his bed to pray, he announced the number of the hymn.

When Johnson stood up to speak, he said, "B. B., don't ever leave us dangling in such suspense again. You told us about your illness, but never did say whether you lived or died."

Johnson's brother, a conductor on the Southern Railroad, had a similar sense of humor. The following story is told by James L. Sullivan of Nashville, who heard it from McKinney when they were in a revival in 1950.

McKinney, like all Sunday School Board employees, traveled many years at reduced fares by invitation of the railroads. En route to an engagement, McKinney was riding on the Southern Railroad when a mammoth-sized conductor came by for his ticket. Recognizing Dr. McKinney, Mr. Johnson decided to have some fun. So he complained, "Just to think—my wife and I go half-starved because we handle preachers at children's rates. We don't even earn enough to feed our children. Preachers, preachers!"

After collecting all the tickets, Johnson wondered if he'd been too hard on McKinney, who had apologized, "I didn't ask for a clergy permit. The railroad just gave me one." So Johnson sat beside him and asked, "Do you know my kid brother, C. Oscar Johnson?"

To which McKinney replied, "Two of a kind!"

There is another beautiful story which I cannot fully document, but merits mentioning. Alta Lee (Grimes) Lovegren, a Southern Baptist missionary to Jordan, heard a testimony "years ago" at Ridgecrest by a man who headed Vacation Bible School Work at the Sunday School Board. She thinks he was Homer L. Grice.

Anyway, this person—whether Grice or not—told at Ridgecrest how McKinney once witnessed to him on a train, leading to his immediate conversion. He reportedly was a railroad porter at the time. Subsequently, he felt a call to a church-related vocation, which led to seminary training and employment at the Board. Alta Lee thinks his name was Grice.

I talked with James L. Sullivan, who has no knowledge of such. However, Grice's biography in the *Encyclopedia of Southern Baptists* (vol. IV, p. 2255) indicates Grice "worked for seven years with the U.S. Railway Postal Service." So there could have been an encounter on a train, and the young man could have been Homer Grice.

There are many examples of McKinney's encouragement of young people. Here are two:

Albert E. and Stewart B. Simms recall how their parents, Mr. and Mrs. Robert N. Simms of Raleigh, North Carolina, began taking them to Ridgecrest in 1931. They went each year for "Preaching Week" when George W. Truett spoke and McKinney directed the music. One year they were assigned the same table in the dining room. The boys remember McKinney, in his deep resonant voice, chanting, "Bread, bread, bread," until the waiters responded.

One summer, when Stewart was nineteen, he tried his hand at writing a song, which McKinney invited him to sing at one of the services. Among

Stewart's mementoes is his original draft of the song, "Closer to Jesus," written on Ridgecrest stationery with hand-drawn lines and spaces. Stewart also has the voucher for a ten-dollar check from the Sunday School Board dated December 23, 1940. McKinney bought the song, although Stewart feels it was never published.

Another example is Wayne R. Maddox, Southern Baptist missionary to Japan, who remembers his first trip to Ridgecrest the summer he was fourteen. The First Baptist Church in Appalachia, Virginia, a small mountain town, had elected Wayne as "song director" and sent him to Ridgecrest for training.

"I knew nothing about music, but was eager to learn," Maddox wrote me from Kyoto, Japan. "When I returned home, I continued to write 'Dr. Mac' in Nashville, cramming a thousand questions into each letter. I was impressed that he answered every letter. That was important to me, as he was my only source of information. Feeling I was taking too much of his time, I suggested in one letter that he might include some music helps in one of the monthly magazines at the Board. Shortly, J. E. Lambdin offered him a 'Church Music Page' in the *Training Union Magazine*."

Walter Hines Sims of Shalimar, Florida, who succeeded McKinney following his death in 1952, says his six years of work with McKinney "were some of the best in my life." He met McKinney in 1928-29 as a student at Southwestern Baptist Seminary, became his associate in 1946, and succeeded him in 1952.

He remembers McKinney as a man with many stories, some of which he told on himself. McKinney's size 12 shoe was always a conversation piece. He told Sims that when traveling by train, he set his shoes outside the Pullman berth at night so the porter could shine them. One morning, he reached for his shoes and discovered the porter had actually shined one shoe and his suitcase!

Sims and McKinney wore the same size 12 shoes and 44 long suits. Once, during a lull at a Southern Baptist Convention in St. Louis, they browsed in a men's clothing store. "A very accommodating salesman waited on us," Sims said. "While I was trying on a suit, I heard the salesman say to McKinney, 'You have a fine son there with you.' I always considered this a compliment. McKinney enjoyed it too, although he didn't correct the salesman. Instead, he thanked him!"

A final example is told by Troy Godwin of Gray Court, South Carolina:

> In 1948 I was pastor of Jordan Street Baptist Church in Greenwood, South Carolina, a small church with 300 members. He came to us from Oklahoma and was real sick with a cold. I took him to my druggist and he gave him something that had him going strong by mid-week.
>
> On the completion of Music Week, he had transferred our struggling choir into a mighty voice for God. Chairs in the aisles, two extra rows for the choir, even put a table out front for Dr. McKinney to stand on to direct his music. Heaven bent low as he led the choir in "When They Ring Those Golden Bells."
>
> Our little church gave him $250 for the week. Not much by today's standards, but at least three times a revival honorarium in those days. He protested, "It's too much; big churches don't do this much for me in revivals." I told him we couldn't pay him for the good he did.
>
> We offered him a motel or hotel but he wanted to stay with us, if it was all right. He had the guest room and ate with us and fell in love with our grammar grade boys, all three of them. He'd watch them play ball. . . . A couple of years later I was with him in a convention at Columbia and we walked over to a variety store where he bought a ball, bat, and glove for me to take home for my sons.

To close this chapter, I'm reproducing McKinney's handwritten letter, accepting Godwin's invitation (which he spelled Goodwin). The letter illustrates McKinney's personal touch. It's probably typical of his correspondence, which he preferred to write in longhand rather than using a secretary.

The letter follows:

The SUNDAY SCHOOL BOARD

of the Southern Baptist Convention

161 EIGHTH AVENUE, NORTH · NASHVILLE 3, TENNESSEE

DIVISION OF
EDUCATION AND PROMOTION
JEROME O. WILLIAMS, SECRETARY
DEPARTMENT OF CHURCH MUSIC
B. B. McKINNEY, SECRETARY
W. HINES SIMS, ASSOCIATE

8. 17-48

Rev James Troy Goodwin,
608 Reynolds Street,
Greenwood S.C.

Dear Friend :

You have tempted me beyond expression. How could I fail to be over in your town sometime this fall? When I think of a good fox chase my blood pressure regesters about twenty degrees higher. It was good of you to ask me to spend a week in your fine Church. Don't see how I can come, but I will. Will try to make a place for the first week in November. Will come or break a trace. Hope the trace holds. Seriously, I will do my best to come to you about the first of November.

Thank you for inviting me.

Yours in Christ
B.B. McKinney

THE
BROADMAN
'PRESS'

The unofficial theme song of Falls Creek Assembly during the 1930s and 1940s, and the all-time favorite of the Bison Glee Club at Oklahoma Baptist University:

Wherever He Leads I'll Go

1. "Take up thy cross and fol-low me," I heard my Mas-ter say;
2. He drew me clos-er to his side, I sought his will to know,
3. It may be thro' the shad-ows dim, Or o'er the storm-y sea,
4. My heart, my life, my all I bring To Christ who loves me so;

"I gave my life to ran-som thee, Sur-ren-der your all to-day."
And in that will I now a-bide, Wher-ev-er he leads I'll go.
I take my cross and fol-low him, Wher-ev-er he lead-eth me.
He is my Mas-ter, Lord, and King, Wher-ev-er he leads I'll go.

Wher-ev-er he leads I'll go, Wher-ev-er he leads I'll go,

I'll fol-low my Christ who loves me so, Wher-ev-er he leads I'll go.

6
"We Always Sing in a Major Key"

Had B. B. McKinney ever adopted a state other than his native Louisiana, surely Oklahoma would have been his choice. Oklahoma was the scene of many, many happy experiences, centered around Falls Creek Baptist Assembly near Davis, as well as Oklahoma Baptist University at Shawnee. First, a look at Falls Creek.

Anyone who's attended a session at Falls Creek knows it defies description, both for size and spirit. Falls Creek, for multiplied thousands, has been an experience more than an event.

McKinney led the singing each summer from 1925 through 1947, with the exception of the war years, 1943-45, when no sessions were held. In 1952, about 1,200 registered. His last year, 1947, attendance reached 11,351. It has continued to grow in succeeding years. During McKinney's years, at least, Falls Creek preserved the early American camp meeting tradition.

Accommodations were primitive in the early years and from 1925 through 1938, he slept in "Tent City." Albert McClellan of Nashville, Tennessee remembers his "little tent as being about 50 yards from the back of the tabernacle. And when he emerged for the services, morning and night, he was tastefully and carefully dressed, usually in white or other light material, rarely wearing a tie. His very presence on the platform put him in control of the music. Once before the crowd, with quiet tones and subdued gestures, he brought them to a spiritual high in preparation for the sermon."

One of McKinney's best friends was E. E. "Hot Dog" Lee, an insurance salesman from Muskogee, Oklahoma who became the first B.Y.P.U. secretary for Indian Territory. Lee, later named national B.Y.P.U. secretary for the Baptist Sunday School Board, taught a huge class at Falls Creek every summer but one from 1917 to 1946. From 1939 on, McKinney shared "Lee's Hut," a private cabin owned by Lee.

In additional to leading the singing at the morning and evening worship services, McKinney taught a 7:15 AM music class in the tabernacle or on a hillside. More than one thousand would attend these informal singalongs.

The folksy way he led these classes is illustrated in a story he enjoyed telling. It was about a church with a paid quartet in which the soprano would lead off with, "As pants." Then the alto would sing, "As pants." The bass and tenor then did the same. Then together the four would sing, "As pants the hart for the mountain brook, so pants my heart for thee, O God." In telling the story, McKinney threw the class into gales of laughter as he mimicked each member of the quartet. In another version, he had each member of the quartet singing, one at a time, "I'll take the pil," then in unison, "I'll take the pilgrim home."

Warren M. Angell of Shawnee, Oklahoma drew me a vivid word picture of Falls Creek in 1936:

> I came to join the faculty at Oklahoma Baptist University in May of 1936, for president John Raley wanted me to meet some of the outgoing students. That August, chemistry professor T. L. Bailey said, "There's a big Baptist meeting at Falls Creek. Dr. Raley's preaching. Would you like to go?"
>
> It was all new to me. I was a Northern Baptist—even Dr. Raley called me a Damned Yankee—they were still fighting the Civil War.
>
> The tabernacle looked like a small barn—it's since been enlarged many times. Folks were camping out all along the creek. No accommodations. We slept on a cot atop a flat-roofed building under the stars.
>
> My, it was hot inside that tabernacle—hotter than the dickens. Fans blowing, stirring up the air. Nearby was a cooking shack, fenced-in like. Raley, a red-headed Irishman, all of 5'6" in his elevated heels, was quite a contrast to big tall McKinney, 6'4" or so.
>
> He had this slow, drawling speech, majestic-like. "We have a

joyful religion and sing everything in the major key," he told us (although I noticed that when he sang *Wayfaring Stranger,* it was in a minor key!). I wasn't too impressed—except I noted everybody was singing.

Angell, who in years to come worked closely with McKinney on his visits to Oklahoma Baptist University as well as at Ridgecrest, goes on to describe the next morning:

At 5 o'clock, everyone was awake, bacon frying, mosquitoes biting. By 6:30, everyone had eaten and was ready for the day. About 7:00, McKinney began a music class on the side of a hill. Looked to me as if everybody was there, a herd of people. No piano, no songbooks. Sang gospel choruses, as well as choruses of familiar hymns. It was like a foreign language to me. The people, sitting on the hillside with small scrub oaks for a background, sang their heads off.

I was amazed at so many there that early and having a good time! "Let's take this song back to our churches," they said, and they did. Between choruses, McKinney kept everyone laughing, especially with his mule stories. They had a different preacher each summer, but insisted McKinney keep coming back.

Folks even came in wagons. Remember, we were just coming out of the worst of the Depression. Others came in trucks, some in broken-down school buses. I was amazed that Baptists would go to a hot hole like that, where the dust never settled, making you cough and sneeze, kicked up by trucks making deliveries and kids playing ball.

But music was it! The singing made everything else worthwhile.

Sunday, I sat next to him on benches while we ate fried chicken dinner off of rough plank tables. It reminded me of camping trips when I was a boy and my Dad took us on camping trips to the woods. We were too poor for tents, so he built a brush arbor with branches on top.

Albert McClellan recalls: "In directing music he never called attention to himself. My friend Orin Cornett, who sang in his choirs in those Falls Creek years, has put it, 'Some song leaders are merely personalities calling for attention. His call was for attention to the song and the Saviour.' The singers 'caught' music from him. The melody was in his soul and it was contagious."

A. L. Greenwalt of Böbingen, West Germany, who attended Falls Creek seven consecutive summers, remembers McKinney saying, "There are two times to sing—when you feel like it, and when you don't feel like it."

And John E. Mathews of Springfield, Missouri recalls the morning McKinney said, "You didn't sing it like I wrote it—but let me hear you sing it again—your way. I want my songs to be the music of the people. Perhaps your way is better. Thank you for helping me write what future generations will sing."

Prudence A. Riffey of Hendersonville, North Carolina says everything didn't always go smoothly at Falls Creek: "One summer the two pianists— one a man, the other a woman—seemed to vie with each other, seeing who could play the most arpeggios and other frills. McKinney later told me in private how he wished they'd give him the notes as written in the hymn-book."

Two of his gospel songs became "trademarks" of Falls Creek during those years. One is "Wherever He Leads I'll Go," which was introduced in the summer of 1936 and sung there for the first time by a large crowd.

Speaking at Ridgecrest in 1974, Eugene Bartlett said he'd seen thousands respond to public invitations at Falls Creek as this number was sung. "And I still get a tingle each time I hear the first few measures," he said.

The second "trademark" is "Glorious Is Thy Name," first published in 1942. J. M. Gaskin, author of *Sights and Sounds of Falls Creek,* told me McKinney led the verses slowly and majestically, "sometimes with both fists clenched and so tall he seemed to touch the ceiling." Then he directed the chorus at a faster tempo. Gaskin lamented that today, the key words in church music are "fast and loud" and that he no longer hears numbers sung the way McKinney directed them.

Gaskin added, "I'm sure he had a private as well as a public self—but his optimism and joy of life spilled over and left a tremendous impression on me. He was warm, human, approachable. He liked cigars—the smoke would just fog out of the cabin he and E. E. Lee shared. (Warren Angell remembers his favorite cigar was a Peter Schuyler, the same brand Angell's father liked.) It was common knowledge he smoked—but that was before the Attorney-General had warned of tobacco. I knew a generation of ministers back then who smoked, many of them from Tennessee. Andrew Potter, our Oklahoma executive-secretary, wouldn't smoke inside a church, but he did out on the lawn."

Gaskin continued, "McKinney thought of himself more as a gospel song writer than a composer of hymns. 'When I Survey the Wondrous Cross' was, to him, the greatest hymn ever written. When he led at Falls Creek, he might stop and take half a minute to describe it, then direct the last verse in a hushed, subdued tone."

Here are other testimonies of those who knew him at Falls Creek:

And those song fests! He had a way of pulling songs out of people. He made you *want* to sing, regardless of whether you felt you could and even if you didn't *feel* like it! He would bend over, extend his long arms downward until his hands almost touched the floor, then, moving his arms in a wide arc, would reach his arms heavenward, stretch upward, standing on tiptoe, and lead in the holds so long I felt my lung would burst!—Mrs. Jerry Lytle, Southern Baptist missionary to Belize, Central America.

The summer of 1928, when I was 12 years old, I decided to ride a bicycle to Falls Creek. It was 60 miles from our home in Shawnee, and only five miles were paved. I left at 6:00 AM and arrived about 1:00 PM. I carried my bedroll and slept under a tent for about 10 days. Dr. McKinney became my boyhood idol. When someone told him I could sing, he asked me to sing "The Old Rugged Cross" at an evening service. I heard him sing "Satisfied with Jesus" just a few months after he'd written it.—George E. Watkins, Griffin, Georgia retired minister of music.

I was in his music class, August 3-10, 1936 and I felt very honored to be there, (yet) I was afraid of him—or should I say that I stood in awe of him. He was a serious man and I was afraid I'd say something I shouldn't. I kept a scrapbook of that precious week, including a faded song sheet mimeographed on the back of stationery from the Immanuel Baptist Church in Tulsa, carrying the name of pastor O. M. Stallings. Included are "He's Done So Much For Me" and the chorus of "Have Faith in God."—Mrs. L. C. Abbott, Corpus Christi, Texas.

When he stretched out his hands to lead us in singing, it was as if he were inviting the whole world to join the song. I realize now that during those Depression years, his optimistic songs meant as much to adults as to us. One afternoon when we all had to run inside our cabins from a rare rain, one group after another could be heard singing, "He sends the rainbow, a lovely rainbow, he sends the rainbow with the rain." We were singing about rainbows; our parents were singing about hope.—Mrs. Boyd Hunt, Fort Worth, Texas.

Since my Dad loved music and directed the Bison Band at O.B.U., we loved to go to Falls Creek. I was only six or seven years old, but I remember the wonderful singing. My two outstanding memories are Dr. McKinney and the Devil's Bath Tub—a natural rock formation where we could swim. I always expected the Devil to pop up any minute!—Mrs. Don (Violet) Orr, Southern Baptist music missionary to Colombia.

Before this album of word pictures draws to a close, I include some insights of J. D. Grey here because they illustrate McKinney's humanness, a trait often revealed at Falls Creek.

Grey tells about the summer of 1937 when he was the guest preacher: "One day after lunch at Falls Creek, he and I walked up the hillside to a grove and sat down on a log, quite a ways from the young people. I took out a cigar and lighted it and he reached under a log for a package of Beech-Nut chewing tobacco. As he put some in his mouth he said, "J. D., this stuff is too good for you to burn up."

Twelve years later, in 1949, Grey and McKinney were in a revival at the

First Baptist Church in Madisonville, Kentucky. Grey was also working on thirteen sermons to be broadcast in April, May, and June on the *Baptist Hour*. "I had told the folks at the Radio Commission in Atlanta that I didn't like the high-brow music they'd been using," Grey told me. "I wanted to use gospel songs, so I asked McKinney to help me. We sat up until nearly midnight each night, while he helped pick out songs to fit my Scripture and topic for a certain Sunday."

In 1950 the two were in another revival at the Immanuel Baptist Church in Paducah, Kentucky. Grey had an elderly aunt by the name of Rubye Orr who lived in a modest farmhouse near Hickory, Kentucky, twelve miles away. She asked Grey to bring McKinney for what she called "a bite to eat."

Grey remembers it as "a very, very humble, poor home, yet B. B. made them feel like he was being entertained in a palace. He sang several numbers as we requested them, which demonstrated to me that here was a warm-hearted person whom people couldn't help loving."

During their times at Falls Creek and in revivals, McKinney told other stories to Grey, such as about the evangelist who asked him in one meeting if it was proper for a song leader to sing his own songs. McKinney replied, "I don't know, but I was with a preacher recently who preached his own sermons." Another evangelist told B. B. that he "would do the preaching and you stick to the singing." Whereupon McKinney said, "Well, I felt like somebody should do *some* preachin' in this meetin'."

The last August that McKinney was at Falls Creek, in 1947, the campers took up a "tub" offering of $874 as a parting gift. "He is now to devote his time to the church music department in Nashville," the congregation was told.

Visitors to Falls Creek today may enjoy the B. B. McKinney Chapel, built in 1964-65 at a cost of $70,000. Constructed of native stone, it was the dream of Gene Bartlett, music secretary for Oklahoma and himself the music director at Falls Creek for years. It has rehearsal facilities for a five-hundred-voice choir and orchestra, music studios, and a historical collection which includes a portable Bilhorn reed organ used at Falls Creek during the early 1930s.

Bartlett started the building fund by donating royalties from his father's song, "Victory in Jesus." The Singing Churchmen of Oklahoma also donated royalties from four of their record albums. Public offerings were taken at the 1962-65 assemblies.

Tulsa architects Joseph Coleman and Leon Ragsdale designed the chapel as a memorial to McKinney, described by Bartlett as "the Stephen Foster of gospel music and my own father in church music." Coleman said:

> The chapel has been designed with sweeping rooflines depicting man's ascent to heaven. Here the horizontal meets the vertical in one majestic movement. Some have suggested that the building literally sings the message of the cross. . . .

By the time the chapel was dedicated in July of 1965, three assemblies were necessary to accommodate the growing crowds. So actually the chapel was dedicated three times—on Thursday night of each of the three weeks. W. Hines Sims, McKinney's successor, was special guest for the first ceremony. Mrs. McKinney came for the second week. Mrs. E. M. Bartlett—Gene's mother—was special guest for the third Thursday night.

Thirteen years later, on August 8, 1978, a historical marker was dedicated at Falls Creek in memory of McKinney and E. E. "Hot Dog" Lee. Gene Bartlett and Mrs. McKinney unveiled it. It's on the site where the "Lee Hut" once stood. Unfortunately, the marker has two errors. It shows McKinney starting at Falls Creek in 1923 instead of 1925. And it states that McKinney wrote "many" of his more than 700 gospel songs in the "Lee Hut." Careful research shows that although McKinney often wrote choruses at Falls Creek, none of his songs in the 1956 or 1975 editions of *Baptist Hymnal* were written there. This "legend" was picked up and freely quoted once the marker was erected. The figure "more than 700 gospel songs" is also an exaggeration. His total writings—published and unpublished—total 501 pieces, including his arrangements of songs by other writers. This is not said to discredit his work, but in the interest of historical accuracy.

Now for Oklahoma Baptist University (O. B. U.) at Shawnee, a second highlight of his career. A lifelong friendship grew from that August 1936 meeting at Falls Creek between McKinney and Warren M. Angell, later to become the dean of the school of fine arts at O. B. U. In subsequent years, McKinney visited the Shawnee campus many times, always the houseguest of president and Mrs. John W. Raley.

When I visited O. B. U. in August of 1984, Mrs. Raley told me:

My grandfather was R. B. Thames, an old storybook Moses-kind of Baptist preacher with a long flowing beard. On his rounds by horseback over Texas, organizing churches, he met E. C. Routh somewhere and took him under his wing. Routh was in our home often while I was growing up. Since his sister later married Dr. McKinney, the name McKinney was a household word.

When we came to O. B. U., our first campus revival was led by L. R. Scarborough and McKinney in 1935. I feel as if I were on the ground floor of emerging professional church music among Southern Baptists in the 1930s. Before that, it was someone merely announcing such and such a page number. Much of the credit is due Angell and McKinney. Angell was from the north—all he knew was paid quartets, paid soloists, paid organists, paid choirs. As a student at Syracuse University, he was organist for Norman Vincent Peale.

So Dr. Raley told McKinney, "We've brought this young man down from New York and you must help him, watch him, talk to him."

Angell had the education, the theory. B. B. had a lifetime of singing in Southern churches. He liked Angell from the start and wrote my husband, "Dr. Raley, you've got a jewel in Angell!"

From 1942-52, McKinney was on our campus nearly every year. He prized the honorary doctorate from O. B. U.—gave him prestige. True, we were a small, emerging school out of the lean 1930s. But Angell began pulling in students from all over, and in 1941 we gave up football to fund our fine arts program.

Our children were little at the time. Although they grew up meeting people, B. B. was special. They felt a kinship to him. Warm to children, he was easy to entertain and cook for.

Raley advised Angell to "get McKinney on campus." So in 1938, two years after the two met in Falls Creek, McKinney came to Shawnee for Oklahoma's first Church Music Conference.

"We invited choir directors from all over the state," Angell told me. "It was sort of a hit and miss affair. I really didn't know McKinney's qualifications. He surprised me by saying he didn't want to do choir work—said for me to do that. He wanted to lead the congregational singing.

"We had no sheet music, so biology professor A. M. Winchester improvised with some tiny Kodak film and we projected words and music on the wall. I painted the wall white and we scooted our chairs up close so we could see. I do choir clinics all over the country, but that's I got my start, in that 1938 conference here in Shawnee."

Angell continued:

> This gave our music department at O. B. U. a start. When I came, only 24 women and one man, an organist, were enrolled. They were just "song heisters" and I had disdain for such. They'd major in religious education, pick up a little song-directing on the side so they could lead music in the churches if they had to. We had some of those hip, hip, hurrah boys who could "lead" but knew little about music.
>
> McKinney and I hit it off from the start. He had the spirit and the personality, and he thought I had the scholarship.

Angell recalls an afternoon at Ridgecrest when the two were sitting in an upstairs room, overlooking the mountains. "What do you think of a college of fine arts right here at Ridgecrest?" McKinney asked. "Something comparable to Westminster Choir School." Angell replied that he thought a degree program in music at all the Baptist colleges would be better.

Still later, McKinney asked Angell if he'd like to come to Nashville, promising, "We'll give you a whole new floor of the Sunday School Board building to train choirs and directors."

As Mrs. Raley indicated, McKinney prized an honorary doctor of music which O. B. U. awarded him in 1942. This occurred during spring commencement, held the night of May 29 in the Shawnee municipal auditorium. U.S. Senator Josh Lee was the speaker. The Women's Glee Club and the Bison Glee Club sang. The combined university and high school bands played the recessional.

Hight C Moore of the Sunday School Board, known for his eloquent writing style, wired Dr. Raley:

EVERYBODY PRESENT IN OUR SUNDAY SCHOOL BOARD PRAYER MEETING THIS MORNING LED BY DR. HOLCOMB VOTED UNANIMOUSLY TO WIRE YOU OUR APPRECIATION OF THE DUE AND DESERVED HONOR WHICH YOUR GREAT UNIVERSITY IS BESTOWING TONIGHT UPON A CHRIST-LIKE AND CONSECRATED COMPOSER OF MANY FAVORITE HYMNS, EDITOR AND AUTHOR OF GREAT GOSPEL MUSIC, POPULAR LEADER OF SOULFUL SONGS IN REVIVALS, AS-SEMBLIES AND CONVENTIONS, TEACHER AND TRAINER OF CHOIRS AND CONGREGATIONS IN THE SONGS OF ZION ON EARTH AS AN EARNEST OF THE CELESTIAL MEL-ODIES IN THE NEW JERUSALEM, OUR BRILLIANT AND BE-LOVED FELLOW WORKER, B. B. MCKINNEY. GOD BLESS HIM AND YOU AND ALL OF US TODAY AND FOR AYE!

And from Nashville, Mrs. McKinney wired:

CONGRATULATIONS TO DOCTOR MCKINNEY. YOU ARE THE BEST AND DEAREST PERSON IN THE WORLD. LOVE, LEILA.

Two years after his death, a certificate of incorporation was filed in Oklahoma City, dated May 27, 1954, for the new B. B. McKinney Music Research Foundation. The bulk of McKinney's papers are deposited with this foundation on O. B. U.'s campus. (See "For Further Reading" for details.)

Although it was not his composition, McKinney sang this wherever he went, including his last public appearance:

The Wayfaring Stranger

Words arr.
Arr. from an old Southern Melody

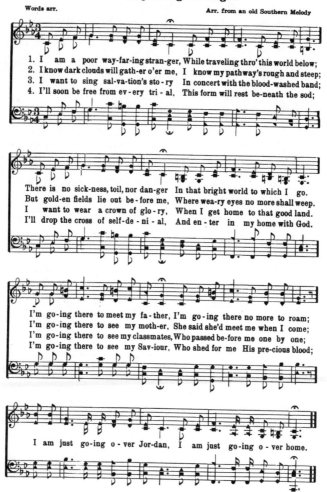

1. I am a poor way-far-ing stran-ger, While traveling thro' this world below;
2. I know dark clouds will gath-er o'er me, I know my pathway's rough and steep;
3. I want to sing sal-va-tion's sto-ry In concert with the blood-washed band;
4. I'll soon be free from ev-ery tri - al, This form will rest be-neath the sod;

There is no sick-ness, toil, nor dan-ger In that bright world to which I go.
But gold-en fields lie out be-fore me, Where wea-ry eyes no more shall weep.
I want to wear a crown of glo-ry, When I get home to that good land.
I'll drop the cross of self-de - ni - al, And en - ter in my home with God.

I'm go-ing there to meet my fa-ther, I'm go-ing there no more to roam;
I'm go-ing there to see my moth-er, She said she'd meet me when I come;
I'm go-ing there to see my classmates, Who passed be-fore me one by one;
I'm go-ing there to see my Sav-iour, Who shed for me His pre-cious blood;

I am just go-ing o - ver Jor-dan, I am just go-ing o - ver home.

7
"I Am Just Going Over Home"

B. B. McKinney died on September 7, 1952, shortly after his sixty-sixth birthday. Tracing his final months, one finds the characteristic pattern of revivals, summer assemblies, and denominational conventions.

There had been discussion between McKinney, T. L. Holcomb, and J. O. Williams about relieving him of administrative details. One possibility was naming his associate, W. Hines Sims, as secretary of the church music department and making McKinney the board's senior music editor. This would give him more time for what he liked—a roving Music Ambassador-at-Large! Office routine had little appeal to him.

Holcomb and Williams were anxious for this transition to be a smooth one, with no overtones of a demotion, for such was not the case.

I made an attempt to trace his steps in 1952, week by week. Since McKinney didn't leave careful records, many gaps are missing. But piecing together bits of correspondence and old program folders, here's what I found:

January of 1952 found him in Columbia, South Carolina, where he led the singing at the state Brotherhood convention.

The University Baptist Church in Carbondale, Illinois, where I was pastor at the time, invited him for a music week, February 11-15. When our music director, Mrs. Harold (Ernestine) Taylor, wrote him a letter of welcome on February 4, she noted that "The only time I've seen you was when I was a little girl and you led the music at the Illinois State Association in my home church in West Frankfort."

In March he led the singing in a revival at the First Baptist Church in Pickens, South Carolina. Nine months later, the December 1952 issue of *The Church Musician* published his chorus "My All for Jesus." Pastor E. R.

Eller immediately wrote Mrs. McKinney that her husband had composed it "one afternoon alone in our kitchen" during that March revival.

We next pick up his trail during the summer when he directed the music, for the last time, at the Alto Frio Baptist Encampment at Leakey, Texas. This assembly is on the Frio River about ninety miles northwest of San Antonio.

McKinney began his annual pilgrimages there about 1944. Frio is Spanish for "high cold," the Frio River being a clear and cold stream.

Allan Cox, now a minister of music in Tyler, Texas, remembers starting to Alto Frio as a boy of eight and watching McKinney rehearse the choir in the old tabernacle. "Later, I'd wave my hands like he did," Cox recalls. When Cox was twelve, he asked McKinney when he could sing in the encampment choir. "Son, get one year older," McKinney promised, but by then McKinney was dead. Cox tells how he learned about McKinney's death on the radio: "When I heard the announcer say he was dead, I cried until I felt I had no tears left. My idol was gone."

Fred W. King, a retired minister in Wharton, Texas, remembers the last time he talked with McKinney:

> We were leaning against a barbed wire fence across the road from Alto Frio. He mentioned his dread of the long trip back to Nashville, by car or bus to San Antonio, and the rest of the way by train. I asked him why he didn't fly. He answered something like this: "I'm having too much trouble with my ears. I have to strain to get the pitch when I'm leading singing, and because of this I seldom sing solos. I'm afraid flying will ruin what little hearing I have left."

Jack Calk, now an associational mission director in the area where Alto Frio is located, has fond memories of first going to camp there when he was thirteen. The church Brotherhood where he was a member paid his expenses of fifteen dollars for winning an essay contest. "I remember sitting spellbound as men like McKinney, Perry F. Webb, and L. H. Tapscott led us," Calk wrote me. "And never do I return to that dear camp without standing and meditating for a few moments, recapturing the magic of those grand days."

That summer McKinney again directed the singing at the thirty-second session of the Paisano Baptist Encampment, also referred to as the Paisano Cowboy Camp Meeting. This was one of his favorite places. It's located in the historic Paisano Pass in the Davis Mountains, between Alpine and Marfar, Texas.

He was there the week of July 21-27, which took on special meaning for him. On his sixty-sixth birthday on July 22, the second day, those present gave him a beautiful wristwatch. Wilburn M. Turner, then pastor of the First Baptist Church in Pecos, was there:

> The gift of his watch on his birthday was the quickest and easiest thing I have ever seen people make possible. He was loved by the Paisano people above all others who have ever been on the grounds, unless it was Dr. Truett, and I doubt that Bro. Mac was loved any less.
>
> Just before he left the platform on the last night to go to Pecos to catch the train, he put his arm around me and said, "Bill, I know you love me. Just remember I love you. I always will."
>
> One of his songs, "I Fell in Love With Jesus," came to him on the grounds at Paisano. He wrote the music while he was in our church in a revival.

Program personnel included Perry F. Webb of San Antonio, F. B. Thorn of Wichita, Kansas, Kyle M. Yates of Houston, and W. R. White of Waco. Sammy Allen, with whom McKinney shared a cabin, made the formal presentation of the birthday watch.

Ten days later found McKinney on the campus of Louisiana College in Pineville for the August 4-8 Church Music Leadership School. Here, forty years earlier, he'd been a student. Todd C. Hamilton, now a Southern Baptist missionary to the Philippines, remembers that at the final session, McKinney called Ernest O. Sellers, then eighty-three, to the front. Asking them to "salute this great man" who had helped him so many summers on the music faculty at Ridgecrest, McKinney presented him "an honorary make-believe bouquet." By the end of the year Sellers had died also.

Seamon Davis of Winnsboro, Louisiana, who was a music director for thirty-five years in three churches, remembers that clinic, too:

I sat in on two of his classes that summer—Vocal Approach and Techniques in Conducting. One day he was asked to lead the blessing at lunch. He raised his hands for all to stand and began to sing the Doxology, "Praise God from whom all blessings flow. . . ." It was heavenly. Since then, when our family gets together for Christmas, Thanksgiving, or homecoming, we stand in a circle, join hands, and sing that. It has become a blessing in our family. We call it the "Davis Blessing."

Probably on that same trip to Louisiana, he stopped at the Louisiana Baptist Children's Home in Monroe for Sunday dinner. There he spoke briefly to the children and led them in some of his choruses, according to a note by D. C. Black in the September 1952 issue of the Home's newsletter.

Sometime that summer, McKinney squeezed in Pioneer Week at the new Glorieta Baptist Conference Center in New Mexico, along with Allen W. Graves, who had co-authored with him, ten years earlier, "Let Us Sing." Graves led the opening prayer. The first Music Week at Glorieta was in 1953, the summer after McKinney's death.

Did McKinney attend his family singing reunion that final summer? Two faded snapshots among the McKinney mementoes tell us he didn't. One shows him getting into a car, topcoat over his arm (indicating early fall weather). On the back is written in longhand, "C. F. Davis taking B. B. to airport at end of last reunion, 1951." The second snapshot is that of his brothers singing around a piano. The handwriting on the back says, "1952 reunion—after B. B. died." These reunions were traditionally near Labor Day—which accounts for the September or October reunion in 1952 after his death.

I've written earlier of these reunions, but more can be said. Winborn E. Davis, the nephew who spent part of his boyhood in the McKinney family residence, says these reunions began in earnest in 1946. In earlier years, relatives would get together to sing and visit whenever B. B. happened to stop by. The reunions continued until 1966, the year before Joanna Davis, who hosted them, passed away.

"These were always picnics at our house," Winborn told me. "A tenant lived in the old family house nearby, and B. B. would always go there to visit, too. Even as a boy, I remember our family songs. They were mostly religious songs, as Mama didn't like what she called hillbilly or Western music.

"All of the McKinney family that I knew enjoyed music—they'd harmonize in four parts. Mama (Joanna) was the organizer, from the start. About 1940, the family organ broke down. A neighbor, who owned a piano 'with real ivory keys' wanted to give it to someone 'who would take care of it.' So she gave us the piano, which we used for the reunions. Each summer, Mama would pay a tuner to come out from Minden to get it ready. Gloria Smith Moore of Coushatta, Louisiana, B. B.'s niece and a daughter of Carrie McKinney Smith, now owns this organ which she's restored and keeps in playing condition."

Winborn remembers one reunion when about forty of them were all singing "When the Saints Go Marching In." He recalls how his Uncle Mac was the "star" of the reunions and didn't like to be upstaged. One afternoon when they were singing "Onward Christian Soldiers," Winborn asked B. B. if he knew the story and proceeded to tell it. B. B. listened without comment. Then abruptly he said, "What else shall we sing?"

James McKinney, a nephew who was for thirty years dean of the School of Sacred Music at Southwestern Baptist Seminary, wrote:

> Despite limited contacts, B. B. was always our favorite uncle and in a sense our hero—our famous relative! One of my favorite memories concerns all the clan gathering around the old pump organ at the John Davis farm near Heflin. Mrs. Davis was B. B.'s sister. As a child, I remember his great love for people and the warmth of his personality.

Gloria Smith Moore played for the reunions during the later years of McKinney's life. "He often told me that if the singer goes in the ditch, you go with him," Gloria told me in a telephone conversation. "He said the accompanist is to follow, not lead, because the singer wouldn't necessarily do a song the way it was written. "I Am a Poor Wayfaring Stranger" was the last song we heard him sing at the 1951 reunion."

Now back to the closing days of the summer of 1952. . . .

B. B. McKinney scheduled one more date on his summer calendar—

Music Week at Ridgecrest, North Carolina, August 26-31. Anticipating a vacation afterward, Mrs. McKinney wrote the Mountain View Hotel in Gatlinburg, Tennessee for a reservation. On August 8 manager Jerry McCutchan wrote her, "We were glad to reserve a third floor room @ $16 a day, American Plan. We shall look forward to serving you." The hotel stationery boasted of "one hundred rooms with bath and steam heat in the shadow of Mt. LeConte with horses and guides available."

Dan Johnson, now with the Board's Church Music Department, remembers McKinney that August "walking around the grounds (of Ridgecrest) in that white, double-breasted suit."

J. Loyd Landrum of Macon, Georgia, a minister of music nearly thirty years, says 1952 was his first Music Week at Ridgecrest. He's always remembered a statement McKinney made, "If you want great congregational singing, love them and lead them."

T. L. Holcomb, who had brought McKinney to the Board in 1935, was the assembly preacher. McKinney came to him during the week and said, "There are many of these people, grown young men and young women, who have never said definitely 'yes' to Christ so far as their life is concerned. They've trusted him as Savior, but have never said, 'You can have my life to use in gospel music, or in the ministry, or to use in any way, anywhere.' I wish we could have one service of dedication."

And they did. McKinney and W. Hines Sims stood at the front to receive those who came. Among the group was Gayle Cameron Griffin who wrote me from Ringgold, Louisiana:

> The summer of 1952, I was 15 and the pianist in the little First Baptist Church of Notasulga, Alabama. Mother decided I would be helped if I could go to Music Week. So she called around to some neighboring churches and arranged for me to go with a group of other young people.
>
> I was overwhelmed by the music, new friends, the classes, the mountains. The Lord dealt with me that week and when I went forward to dedicate my life, the person who met me and led me to the counseling room was B. B. McKinney. He told me that if I chose church music, it would be a life of practice, practice, prac-

tice. I don't remember everything he said. I do remember the love expressed in his voice. That was my brief but life-changing encounter with him.

Gayle returned for other music weeks, majored in music at Oklahoma Baptist University and married a student preacher at Southwestern Baptist Seminary. "I've continued ever since to use my talent in music for the Lord," she concluded.

His last known composition was "My All for Jesus," which he had written in March in Pickens, South Carolina. He apparently introduced it at Ridgecrest in August, giving the manuscript copy to Martha Lou Summerall, who had accompanied his classes. William G. Stroup, now of Jacksonville, Florida, wrote me that Martha took the copy home to Crystal Springs, Mississippi. There, the very next week, it was sung in a revival in the First Baptist Church. Stroup forwarded a copy to Loren Williams at the Sunday School Board, who reproduced it in the December 1952 issue of *The Church Musician:*

> My all for Jesus,
> My all for Jesus,
> No other Master
> My heart shall know;
> Today, tomorrow,
> In joy or sorrow,
> My all for Jesus
> Who loves me so.

Estimates of attendance at Ridgecrest that week vary from 1,500 to 3,000. Whatever the total, McKinney was surely gratified to see how Music Week had grown from that first handful in the 1930s.

On Thursday night, by request, he sang "I Am a Poor Wayfaring Stranger," one of his "trademarks." It was the last solo he sang. It was also the last number his relatives had heard at the family reunion the preceding summer. The words "I am just going over home" proved to be prophetic.

The Friday night service was given over to the songs he composed. On Saturday night, a four-hundred-voice choir presented Mendelssohn's *Elijah*. On Sunday night, they gave Handel's *The Messiah* directed by Dupre Rhame. At the close, McKinney was asked to come down to the front from the balcony, where he'd been sitting, to lead the benediction. Uriel Powell of Roanoke Rapids, North Carolina, who was present, said he "prayed for a safe journey for all." Eugene F. Quinn remembers him telling the audience to "be careful on your way home." It was his last public appearance.

Most people left for home the next morning, Labor Day. McKinney told a friend he and Leila were staying until Tuesday as it "wasn't safe to drive in the mountains on a holiday weekend."

Five years earlier, in 1947, he had sat at the breakfast table of Troy Godwin in Greenwood, South Carolina. There he told Godwin, his friend, of a foreboding fear of automobile accidents.

As the McKinneys pulled out of the assembly grounds on Tuesday morning, headed for the Mountain View Hotel in Gatlinburg, they stopped to say goodbye to Willard K. "Daddy" Weeks, assembly manager. Weeks is the last known person to talk with McKinney, aside from Leila.

It was raining in the mountains and on a sharp curve near Cherokee, North Carolina, their car spun out of control. Somehow the door on the driver's side sprang open and McKinney fell to the pavement. The *Waco* (Texas) *News-Tribune* reported that he was run over by his own car as well as the one following close behind. A third car crashed into the wreckage. He suffered nine broken ribs and a punctured lung, plus head and chest injuries. Mrs. McKinney was not hurt.

One of the motorists who stopped took him to the County Hospital in Bryson City, North Carolina. He was William D. Nix of Asheville, North Carolina. One account indicates he was a physician.

The McKinneys' two sons came to his bedside, as well as Dr. and Mrs. W. Hines Sims. Other visitors included Rev. and Mrs. Ewell Payne and one of their sons from the Indian Baptist mission in Cherokee.

Porter W. Routh of Nashville, a nephew of Mrs. McKinney, said:

> I shall never forget the hot day in September of 1952 when Aunt Leila called and told me that Uncle Mac was near death. I got a plane immediately to Knoxville where pastors Ramsey Pollard and W. W. Warmeth had a car at the airport for me to drive over to Bryson City.
>
> When I walked into the hospital, a young red-headed doctor

(William D. Mitchell), perspiration streaming down his face, was just coming out of the operating room. I introduced myself and asked how Mr. McKinney was doing. He told me the promise was not good, then added, "I've never been through such an experience. All the time we were trying to give him transfusions, he was trying to lead us in a choir rehearsal."

Similar reports came from other persons. According to Young H. Walker of Old Fort, North Carolina, B. B. was "seen to be beating time to music that others present couldn't hear." Cloyd A. Adcox of Orlando, Florida, who worked thirty-six years in the Nashville post office and knew McKinney well, wrote me that he was heard to say, "Let's sing that chorus one more time."

Mrs. L. M. (Mary) Jackson of Winston-Salem, North Carolina, was one of the area persons who drove to the hospital to express concern. Family members told her that at one time, McKinney was singing hymn after hymn, although unconscious. And periodically, he stopped as if to listen, then whispered, "I don't know that song. Sing it again so I can learn it." Others said he tried to sing snatches of Handel's "Hallelujah Chorus."

In the McKinney collection at the Dargan Research Library in Nashville is a packet of thirteen cards signed by thirteen GAs from the First Baptist Church in Bryson City. Each is lettered with a Bible verse, and some include the title of one of his hymns. They took these to Mrs. McKinney at the hospital, as a reminder of their concern during her five days of waiting. Helen M. Gibson of Bryson City, their leader at the time, wrote me in 1984, recalling what her girls did. "We also copied some of his hymns and arrangements for Mrs. McKinney to read," she added.

From Nashville on September 2 came a wire from Clifton J. Allen at the Board: "Group has just met in my office earnestly praying for Dr. McKinney and you. Our love and prayers continue. Romans eight twenty-eight."

Confident that all things *do* work for good to those who love the Lord, friends and relatives gave up their Mr. Music Ambassador-at-Large on Sunday, September 7.

At 1:09 that afternoon, T. L. Holcomb sent wires to Baptist leaders throughout the nation: "B. B. McKinney passed away at noon today in Bryson City hospital. Funeral will be Tuesday afternoon in Nashville."

A funeral ambulance from Finley-Dorris & Charlton Home in Nashville drove to Bryson City to return his body. And on Tuesday afternoon, September 9, at 3:00 PM, services were held at the First Baptist Church in Nashville, where he and Mrs. McKinney had been members since 1936.

Pastor W. F. Powell, T. L. Holcomb, and John L. Hill officiated. Minister of music D. Neil Darnell directed the church choir in singing two of his compositions—"Have Faith in God" and "Wherever He Leads I'll Go." The choir also sang "Near the Cross," which he once told Charles W. Horner of Anderson, South Carolina, was his favorite hymn.

G. Kearnie Keegan sang "Satisfied with Jesus," which McKinney considered his best work. Only he changed the wording of the last verse:

> And *his* work on earth is ended,
> And *he* crossed the mystic sea,
> And *he* does hear Him saying,
> "I am satisfied with thee."

C. A. Holcomb remembers flowers "banked three and four deep across the entire front of the church." One wreath was in the shape of a musical lyre. Across it was a wide ribbon on which read, "Have Faith in God." The card was signed, Oklahoma Church Music Family.

Burial was in Woodlawn Memorial Park in Nashville.

Mrs. McKinney said she received over 1,200 letters and cards, many from people she had never met. Some typical ones:

> He was truly a man of God, talented, dedicated, humble.— Maxey Jarman when presenting a citation to Mrs. McKinney from the Good News Class, First Baptist, Nashville.

> When I read of his death, it was like losing a personal friend.— Elsie E. Paddock, Oxnard, California.

> Remember what he said at Falls Creek—"When you preachers get to heaven, you'll be without a job, but I can keep on singing."—Alice McKinney.

Though the voice of the singer has been stilled, the music of his life shall live forever.—John W. Raley, Shawnee, Oklahoma.

Mac's going was a coronation experience.—E. C. Routh, Lockhart, Texas.

A great host here at Buckner Orphans Home feel great loss in the homecoming of Big Brother.—Robert C. Buckner and family, Dallas.

Deep sorrow has settled on us. Dear old Mack has gone.—C. S. Cadwallader, Duback, Louisiana.

We will all miss him and his great contribution to gospel music. A great chorus will be waiting to sing with him. Christ has made of death but a narrow starlit strip between the communion of yesterday and the reunion of tomorrow.—Homer Rodeheaver, Winona Lake, Indiana.

News . . . reached us just as we were to begin another service in citywide campaign here in Pittsburgh. Our hearts were wonderfully moved as we sang some of his great songs. We thank God for every memory of the man who gave us our theme chorus, "Send a Great Revival in My Soul."—Billy Graham and team, Pittsburgh, Pennsylvania.

We can be happy in the blessed assurance of his own happiness. I'll never quit being grateful for the priceless privilege of being so intimately with him in the work.—E. E. Lee, Covington, Georgia.

One of the most touching messages is a three-page letter from his sister Carrie, the one he confided in as a youth that he "was writing little songs but tore them up before anyone could see." It's a warm, personal letter on plain paper, compared with many typewritten ones on stationery. The letter thanked Leila for kindness shown while she was in Nashville for the funeral. She closes, "Well, Leila, I can't write nice and well-worded letters, but this will let you know we are thinking about you and praying for you. We will always love you." In spite of her protests, the letter is neat and well worded. B. B. would have been proud of her plainness, for his faith was rooted in the simple life of a Louisiana farm family.

The Sunday School Board held a memorial chapel service on September 12. On December 7, the nationwide *Baptist Hour* broadcast a special of his music, including "Satisfied with Jesus," sung again by G. Kearnie Keegan.

Reports came from many churches throughout the Southern Baptist Convention which held special Sunday evening services that fall, using McKinney music exclusively.

Of everything her husband wrote, this was Mrs. McKinney's favorite:

Have Faith in God

1. Have faith in God when your path-way is lone-ly, He sees and
2. Have faith in God when your pray'rs are un-an-swered, Your ear-nest
3. Have faith in God in your pain and your sor-row, His heart is
4. Have faith in God tho all else fail a-bout you; Have faith in

knows all the way you have trod; Nev-er a-lone are the
plea he will nev-er for-get; Wait on the Lord, trust his
touched with your grief and de-spair; Cast all your cares and your
God, he pro-vides for his own; He can-not fail tho all

least of his chil-dren; Have faith in God, have faith in God.
Word and be pa-tient, Have faith in God, he'll an-swer yet.
bur-dens up-on him, And leave them there, oh, leave them there.
king-doms shall per-ish, He rules, he reigns up-on his throne.

Have faith in God, he's on his throne; Have faith in God, he watches o'er his own;

He can-not fail, he must pre-vail; Have faith in God, have faith in God.

Words and tune MUSKOGEE, B. B. McKinney, 1934. Copyright 1934. Renewal 1962. Broadman Press. All rights reserved.

8
"She's Mine, If I Can Get Her!"

Since Mrs. B. B. (Leila Irene Routh) McKinney is a legend in herself, out-living her composer-husband by thirty-three years, I've chosen to devote an entire chapter to her.

Chapter 2 has already described that November afternoon in 1916 when B. B., seated on the platform at the First Baptist Church in Waco, Texas, saw Leila in the congregation and vowed, "She's mine, if I can ever get her." Now, let's review earlier details.

Leila was born December 28, 1899 on her parents' farm in the Plum Grove Community, Fayette County, Texas. Her parents were Joseph E. Routh and Mary E. (Stramler) Routh. They were members of the Plum Grove Baptist Church (the third Missionary Baptist church organized in all of Texas). Leila had one brother, fifteen years older than she. He was E. C. Routh, later the editor of *The Commission* Magazine in Richmond, Virginia as well as two Baptist state papers—the *Baptist Standard* in Texas and the *Baptist Messenger* in Oklahoma.

Six months after Leila was born, her father, Joseph, died of malarial he-maturia. Mary Routh, determined to stay on the farm, found a cousin to come live with her and six-month-old Leila. The teenage son, E. C. Routh, was already away in school and she resisted all advice to "bring your boy home and let him run the farm."

Leila remembers those early years on the farm and how hard her mother worked to keep the agreement she and Joseph had made to give both children a college education.

"Mother canned fruits and vegetables all summer," Leila said. "We had grape vines, peach, pear, plum, and fig trees, plus all kinds of vegetables. We drew water from a deep well and heated it in a tank on the back of the cookstove.

"We did have some valuable colored help—Rachel and her sister Jane. They came and built fires in the backyard on wash day and hog-killing time. Mother gave them a little cash money and their dinner. They boiled the clothes and helped make sausage, lye soap, and lard. They were our friends. If everyone were as fair as Mother, there'd be no race problems today.

"I remember our pretty front yard with all of Mother's roses. She showed me lots of love. But as my only parent, she had to discipline me. She kept a switch—oh, how it hurt!"

Leila quickly learned money management one Christmas when she received one dollar to buy presents. After spending eighty-five cents on a favorite cousin, she came back to her mother for more—but didn't get it. "Mother told me to learn to buy with what I had."

When Leila was six years old, her mother married John W. Wroe, a deacon in the Winchester Baptist Church at nearby Winchester, Texas. Although they moved to his home in Winchester, Leila's mother kept and rented the farm.

"Mother and my stepfather kept their money separate, because she had property from her first marriage and was a careful manager," Leila remembered. "There were no bank accounts or credit cards then, so Mother buried her money in a jar—paid for all my schooling.

"When I was about eight, she paid cash for a new piano. I remember when it was delivered by wagon from the county seat. Mother hired a teacher who came to our home. She made me practice, because she'd saved for that piano! I loved music, but I didn't always want to practice. I liked to play outside."

Growing up in Winchester, Leila heard Baptist and Methodist preaching once a month, and Presbyterian sermons less often. At the age of fourteen or fifteen, she accepted Christ and joined the Methodist church—by immersion, at her insistence!

Her mother's dream for college came true in the fall of 1905 when Leila entered Baylor Female College, now the University of Mary-Hardin Baylor.

She remembers how her brother, E. C. Routh, went along to "sign me up" for four years of Greek and four years of Latin. She resented it at the time, thinking he was "dictating" to her.

However, she developed a love for languages and in her third year of Greek, after studying the New Testament in the original language, she became convinced she should be a Baptist. In the fall of 1908 her brother, E. C., baptized her at the First Baptist Church in Belton, Texas. She graduated in 1909, then came home to Winchester where she gave private piano lessons for three years.

One year when she was in college, boll weevils ruined the crops and the tenant asked her mother for a year's grace to pay. Since he'd made no money either, her mother forgave his debt and immediately sent Leila to a friend to borrow the tuition. Leila's mother told her exactly what to say.

Leila was pleased when she got the loan, with no written agreement. As promised, it was repaid the next year.

Leila's interest in Greek continued well beyond college. Years later, when she lived in Nashville, she and her pastor, F. Franklin Paschall, and one other person met one morning a week in her home to read the Greek New Testament. They did so for about six years.

Leila's mother continued to encourage her quest for education, so in the fall of 1912 she entered Baylor University in Waco, Texas and earned a second bachelor of art degree in 1913.

She then taught Greek and math for a year at Rusk Baptist Junior College at Rusk, Texas, plus a year at Goodnight, Texas Junior College, also a Baptist school. Then followed four years as a Latin teacher at Mary Hardin-Baylor College, during which she met her future husband.

Although Leila had studied piano, her first interest was languages. For one reason, she was tone deaf and couldn't "hear" the music she was playing.

Before she married, Leila asked a college teacher if she'd take her on as a voice student. "I knew my efforts at singing didn't sound musical," she said in later years. "At the end of the quarter, my grade was C and I felt I didn't deserve even that. Because Mother had sacrificed to send me to college, I'd made special efforts to make good grades. But now a C! Can you imagine how I felt?"

Leila asked her voice teacher for a frank opinion and got it: "I believe you should major on piano."

This she did. After she and B. B. were married, she studied a year at

Texas Christian University in Fort Worth where she earned a bachelor's degree in music.

"I can't sing a note," Leila told me. "Mac married me in spite of it. So although I couldn't sing with him, I could play the piano while he sang. He didn't seem disturbed that I couldn't sing. I still can't! But I sometimes 'hymn' to myself. I accompanied him at all kinds of meetings and was one of the pianists for worship services at Travis Avenue Church. Sometimes he'd say, 'Leila, come and play this for me,' or 'Listen to how this sounds.' I don't think he ever wrote anything he didn't ask me to play.

"I often envied Mac that he could write hymns and I couldn't. It was a gift. His writing was an overflow of his love for the Lord. His aim was to please Him, not just compose a song. And his chief joy was revival music. George W. Truett had him many times for revivals in Dallas. He'd come home exhausted from a meeting, but filled with reports of people blessed and saved. He went a 'jillion' places to sing. When he returned from a week at Falls Creek, he'd be ten pounds lighter."

Just as Leila filled a need in McKinney's life, so he met a need in hers. For one thing, he bolstered her self-confidence. She hesitated when C. E. Matthews offered her a job on the staff as Training Union director at Travis Avenue Church, since she had no seminary training. B. B. reassured her there wasn't "anything on earth she couldn't do, once she decided." And succeed she did in that job, as well as a similar one after they moved to Nashville.

"When he was away from home, Mac wrote me every day," she said in a magazine interview. "On weekends, he always sent me special delivery letters. After he was gone, when I would hear the kids with one of those play (toy) whistles, I'd break down and cry. It reminded me of the special delivery letters he sent me. I didn't see why he couldn't be spared to keep on serving the Lord. It was really hard for me. I was rebellious about it. . . . I couldn't understand. For a time, I couldn't pray 'Thy will be done.' Once again, Mac's confidence helped. I felt like he would expect me to carry on."

For years, Leila carried in her purse a letter he wrote her one Friday before Mother's Day. When I began work on this biography, I asked her son, Baylus, Jr., if he could furnish me with a copy. He did, and here's how it reads. The letter is undated, but I'm estimating the late 1930s. He wrote from Decatur, Georgia on stationery of the Hotel Candler:

Friday PM

Just from town and couldn't resist sending this Mother's Day card to the most precious mother in all the world, my sweetheart and mother of my precious boys. No words can express my deep appreciation and love for your beautiful life of devotion to your home and your three boys. You have never failed us in any way. Your unselfish life is a rebuke to me, but (also) a wonderful example to follow. I love you sincerely and am happier every day to call you my own. Love and kisses. Wish I could be with you Sunday. Yours forever and ever, Dad.

No wonder she often said, "For Mac and me it was a romance and *is* a romance."

Leila's contribution to the lives of others reached a climax in the twelve years she was Training Union director at the First Baptist Church in Nashville, 1937-1949. She was offered the job at a modest seventy-five dollars a month about a year after they moved to Nashville. What she accomplished during those years is legendary, not only in boosting attendance on Sunday evenings, but touching the lives of hundreds of servicemen during World War II.

Aware of the large number of military personnel in area training centers, and looking for something to relieve anxiety about her own two sons away at war, she sponsored what she called a Fellowship Hour for refreshments and getting acquainted on Sunday nights after church. Although she said she faced "some resistance" from the deacons, the idea took hold. At first only youth came; then adults joined in and it took on the atmosphere of a community event.

But that wasn't all. She also:

• Put up a special bulletin board for snapshots, letters, and clippings from and about servicemen.

• Ran errands for them in Nashville, such as birthday and Christmas shopping, setting aside one cabinet in her office just for them.

• Had out-of-town service people in her home for meals and weekends.

• Wrote the parents of every first-time visitor to say their son was in church, plus made countless phone calls to many of them.

• Sometimes sat up until 3 AM writing personal letters to those overseas, reinforced with Valentines, birthday cards, and Christmas greetings.

• Published items in the church bulletin under "Training Union" notes, such as: "Lt. Raymond Tyler, consecrated and gifted member, will not be coming home. He died in a plane crash in England. . . . Pvt. Floyd Reeves was seriously wounded in Guam. Pfc. James Hart and Pfc. William Hart both wounded in France, hospitalized in England."

And starting in late 1944, she wrote and mailed a five-page newsletter to over five hundred servicemen whose names she'd compiled from local members plus young men who had visited on Sunday nights.

Were these efforts appreciated? After Dr. McKinney died in 1952, one of her sympathy letters came from Charles J. Julian of Algood, Tennessee. He mentions when his son, Tom, was on the church prayer list, apparently in World War II:

> And it was a great consolation that Tom was saved and had the very happy pleasure of seeing him baptized there. Tom assured me in several letters that he was saved and for me not to worry if he did not come home. . . . I was baptized about a year ago this month and am very happy in the Lord's work, trying to teach the men's Bible class."

From Marietta, Georgia I received a March 29, 1985 letter from Harold E. Graham, Sr. A graduate of Southern Baptist Seminary in Louisville, Graham said he'd been a missions director in eight associations and "had a part in starting about one church a year." He wrote:

> In Oct., 1943, I came face-to-face with the reality of my lostness. I was among hundreds of servicemen in a replacement depot in Nashville to prepare for special overseas combat. Knowing I was lost without hope, I locked myself in an empty barracks, prayed for salvation, and was saved.
>
> Whereupon I made my way to the old First Baptist Church seeking baptism. There I met the McKinneys! They embraced this homesick 24-year-old Savannah, Georgia boy, assured me of Christ's love and their love. They gave me an inscribed New Testament, dated Oct. 16, 1943, which I carried around the world and which I treasure to this hour.

illiterate; urging the good to be better and interesting the bad to be good; pointing and leading the way onward and upward. God bless you and all dear to you today and for aye!

Each December, she hosted a dinner for the state music directors who came to Nashville to meet with Dr. McKinney and W. Hines Sims. She recalled: "On the morning they were coming that evening, I arose very early and baked two angel food cakes. We had a part-time maid, a Southern gentlewoman, a great Christian, and she helped me prepare the fried chicken and hot biscuits."

After his death, Leila often quoted what McKinney had written in the October 1950 issue of *The Church Musician*.

> We need to use hymns and gospel songs that will lead lost souls to Christ, practical hymns and gospel songs that are doctrinally sound . . . that will provide help and comfort in dark hours, organ and choir music that the average person in the congregation will understand and enjoy, good anthems that will reach the heart of the unsaved as well as the redeemed.

About five years after McKinney's death, Leila set out on a project to accumulate copies of everything he'd written. This was not easy. William J. Reynolds, who assisted her, fills in the details:

> I was glad to help her with this as we searched for obscure songs that had been printed only once. She did a remarkable job. We mounted the individual songs on heavy paper and then microfilmed them. A positive print went to all Southern Baptist seminary libraries. Mrs. McKinney then had everything bound into three handsome volumes and they were presented to Oklahoma Baptist University, which had established the B. B. McKinney Foundation.
>
> These bound volumes provide the best source for determining the quantity of his output. I suggested we organize the material into these five categories:
>
> (1) Songs for which he wrote both words and music: 187.

And E. Harvey Walworth, Southern Baptist missionary to Mexico wrote me on March 26, 1984 from Mobile, Alabama that Mrs. McKinney has been a strong influence for good in his life. Harvey met her "when was a young soldier stationed at Smyrna Air Force Base near Nashville."

Although she gave up her Training Union work in 1949, she continued her "birthday ministry." Each December she bought a little red address book at Kress Department Store to keep her birthday prayer list of over eight hundred names.

"My stamp bill is horrible," she once lamented to Normal Jameson for a *Baptist Press* interview. "I do without a new dress to buy stamps."

W. Howard Bramlette of Nashville wrote me that what he remembers most warmly about Mrs. McKinney was her birthday telephone calls. "Somehow we never expected the call, but we knew it was a habit of hers, and it was a special blessing for her to say she was remembering you in prayer," he told me. "She must have done this for decades."

And H. S. Simpson of Nashville recalled how as a ten-year-old boy back in 1924 on Seminary Hill, he got a birthday call from Mrs. McKinney.

Describing his years as a student in Nashville and part-time employee at the Baptist Sunday School Board, James H. Cox of Middletown, Kentucky told me the five members of his family got birthday calls, year after year. "It would never have seemed like our birthday if we hadn't heard from Mrs. Mac," he said. "I used to be amazed how this little old grandma zipped around town in her Volkswagen. The two seemed inseparable! In my days of youth she seemed awfully old, but nothing seemed to thwart her."

Jack Porter of Raleigh, North Carolina wrote me of his friendship with Leila when he was a Nashville student, 1946-49. "We saw Dr. McKinney less often," he added. "I've always been amazed at a testimony he told u one evening—that in the face of all his accomplishments, he was never abl to read music." And Carr M. Suter wrote from Garland, Texas recallin several Sunday dinners with the McKinneys when he was a student Vanderbilt University, 1945-48.

No wonder that in 1949, Hight C Moore authored this resolution to Le on behalf of the church:

Everyday Friend of Everybody Everywhere,
old and young; rich and poor; famous and obscure; learned and

(2) Songs for which he wrote original music for words by other authors: 151.

(3) Songs for which he wrote original music for music by other composers: 16.

(4) Arrangements of songs by other writers: 113.

(5) Original choral anthems: 13.

(6) Arrangements of choral anthems: 21.

Adding these five categories, Mrs. McKinney's collection of his works of all kinds totals 501.

One of the last things Leila did in Nashville was to witness B. B. McKinney's induction into the Gospel Music Hall of Fame. This was done at the thirteenth annual Dove Awards Presentation in Nashville on March 3, 1982. Leila was then ninety-two years of age. Other inductees, through 1984, include such musicians as George Beverly Shea, Ralph Carmichael, G. T. "Dad" Speer, Fanny Crosby, Mahalia Jackson, Ira Sankey, E. M. Bartlett, Homer Rodeheaver, and Ethel Waters.

1982 also saw Leila move out of the Nashville house at 1605 Cedar Lane which had been her home since early 1936. In failing health, she was moved to Morningside Manor at 602 Babcock Road in San Antonio, Texas. Both of her sons live in San Antonio.

On August 14-15, 1983, Mrs. Hastings and I spent two long mornings with Mrs. McKinney in the retirement center. We learned little we didn't already know from research and response to ads placed in the state Baptist papers and from relatives, but we did benefit from insights and the warmth of her personality that has flavored this entire book.

While there, I also talked with her sons, Baylus, Jr., and Eugene. I have already quoted in chapter 2 from Baylus, Jr., who retired in 1966 after a twenty-five-year career in the Army Air Force as a navigator-bombadier on the B-47 (forerunner of the B-52). Baylus, Jr. went to Hardin-Simmons University on a scholarship as a member of the famed Cowboy Band and traveled extensively with it. Following military service, Baylus, Jr. was a band director in junior and senior high schools.

Eugene, who graduated from Baylor University in Waco, Texas, later taught playwriting at Baylor as well as the Dallas Theater Center and Trinity University in San Antonio. A member of the Writers Guild of America, he has produced screenplays as well as television scripts for NBC, ABC, and CBS. He filled me in on additional details about his Dad:

> When we lived in Nashville, I'd stop in his office when I was downtown for a movie, and we'd go out to eat. One day, in a greasy spoon kind of restaurant, a waiter thanked Dad for "doing the best thing that ever happened to me." I learned he had signed probation papers or a petition to get that waiter from prison.
>
> If Dad ever had a fault, I don't know it. He never fell from the pedestal, at least in my sight. He's an unbelievable person. I can't use him in my plays. I can Mother, for I see her objectively. Her I. Q. was double that of Dad's. Without her drive and ambition, he probably would have been an itinerant musician.
>
> She's tone deaf—can't "hear" what she's playing. I've never heard her sing a note, even in congregational singing. No wonder she didn't want to practice piano as a little girl.
>
> I did use him briefly in one of my plays, "A Different Drummer," the episode about a girl riding piggy-back, playing like it was a train. The description of her father is actually my father. I vividly remember being bounced on Dad's knee—and he could make great train whistles with his hands!

Three performances of "A Different Drummer" were presented at Southwestern Baptist Seminary in Fort Worth in October of 1983, directed by Darrel Baergen. During the performances, the boyhood home of Eugene and Baylus, Jr. at 4505 Frazier on Seminary Hill was pictured.

As we talked on, Eugene told me more:

> Dad could have been moderately wealthy, had he better controlled his work. After he went to the Baptist Sunday School Board, I remember him being paid, for his previous work, a $17.50 monthly royalty (in addition to salary), plus $2.50 a month royalty on "foreign" use of his works.
>
> At his death, the Board paid Mother $900 for rights to all songs

copyrighted by him before 1936. While at the Board, his creative work was considered "for hire" under the copyright laws. In all fairness, however, he did much of his composing on Board time.

In retrospect, I see him as somewhat naive. He came along at the right time in the denomination with an emphasis on basic, singable music. He was not a bureaucrat, a politician, an administrator. The complex organization at the Board wouldn't fit him today. He worked on a one-to-one basis. I don't see him administering a complex system with organization charts, computer printouts of budget, and the like. And today's youth musicals would probably be too jazzy for his tastes.

While in San Antonio, I also talked with Henry C. McGill, Jr., M.D., a boyhood chum of Eugene McKinney in Nashville. "I was in the McKinney home once or twice a week," McGill told me. "I remember Gene's dad as a gentle, warm, reserved person. Not talkative. I also observed him when he led the singing in our church. He was reserved and restrained in his gestures as he was in speech. He made few comments, and never sermonized. He wasted no motion in his song-directing. As a teenager in their home, I wasn't aware he was a composer. He didn't volunteer information about himself."

I cherish our last morning with Mrs. McKinney in San Antonio. Although her memory was fading and she sometimes got names and dates mixed, B. B. McKinney was real. "When Mac was gone," she said, "everything became dark. I couldn't conceive living without him. I never get tired of talking about Mac—from now to doomsday."

Mrs. Hastings was with me both mornings, and we didn't want the time to come to say good-bye to her. Both mornings she had worn a dark rose, crepe dress, her hair pulled back into a bun, held in place with silver-colored pins. She wore matching earrings and a hearing aid. Her dress, frilly at the neck and wrists, was trimmed with a gold braid. She wore silver-rimmed glasses, gold-colored beads, a gold pin on her dress, and black oxfords (dressy type) laced neatly.

The last day she carried a Bible, the August 8 issue of *Time* Magazine, the morning newspaper, the current issue of *The Commission*, which her brother had once edited, and an umbrella.

"The paper speaks of rain," she said, explaining the umbrella. It was apparent she was planning to leave with us. She knew we had something to do with the Dargan Research Library in Nashville. She knew that many of Mac's mementoes were there, which she wanted to see again.

Watching me make final notes, she said, "Be sure to write down the sweetest name of all—your wife's!" So, I write her name now, Bessie, who helped with my research in Nashville, visited Mrs. McKinney with me, and typed this manuscript.

We escorted her down a hallway for our final walk together. She complimented two women on their hairstyles. She spoke warmly to an orderly who was mopping the floor, and commented to me, "I know where I am—it's San Antonio."

A nurse's aide who had sensed Mrs. Mac's intention to go with us suggested to me that it would be better if we just slipped out while Leila was in the bathroom. I felt this was rude, so I kissed her on the forehead and said we were leaving while the aide gently held onto her arm.

Tears came to our eyes as we pulled out of the driveway, for we were certain we would never see her again on this earth.

Leila Routh McKinney died in her sleep about two years later, on March 1, 1985. Her body was returned to Nashville for funeral services at the First Baptist Church, as they had been for her Mac in 1952. And as you'd expect, all of the music was from the pen of her gifted husband.

Somewhere in this story of Mac and Leila, I wanted to include one sample of his work in his own handwriting. Such a sample appears on page 149. Actually, it's not the original manuscript for "Thanks Be to God," copyrighted 1947. Rather, it's a transposition he did for a Thanksgiving Day service in my home church, First Baptist Church in Marion, Illinois.

McKinney was there for a revival and wanted to sing this at the Thanksgiving service. So he transposed it into the key of C for organist Lillian Collier, who loaned it for reproduction here.

So, for me, the story nears its end on a beautiful nostalgic note. For I knew B. B. McKinney. And many, many Sundays as a boy, I enjoyed the music of our church organist, Lillian Gore Collier.

Thanks Be to God.

B.B.M⁚K

B. B. McKinney

Thanks be to God for life and light For love and joy and sun-shine bright; For grace to lead us thro' the night Thanks be to God, thanks be to God!

Chorus.

Thanks be to God, thanks be to God! For wood-land and mead-ow For life-giv-ing sod, For bless-ings un-numbered, our paths we have trod, Thanks be to God, Thanks be to God!

An example of how McKinney wrote or adapted a song to meet a specific human need:

When the Morning Comes

1. Tri - als dark on ev - 'ry hand, And we can - not un - der- stand
2. Oft our cher-ished plans have failed, Dis - ap-point-ments have pre-vailed,
3. Temp - ta - tions, hid - den snares Of - ten take us un - a - wares,

All the ways that God would lead us to that bless - ed promised land;
And we've wandered in the dark-ness, heav - y - heart - ed and a - lone;
And our hearts are made to bleed for some tho't-less word or deed,

But he'll guide us with his eye, And we'll fol - low till we die; We will
But we're trust-ing in the Lord, And, ac - cord-ing to his Word, We will
And we won - der why the test When we try to do our best, But we'll

un - der-stand it bet - ter by and by. By and by, when the morn - ing

comes, When the saints of God are gath - ered home, We will tell the sto - ry

How we've o - ver-come; We will un - der-stand it bet - ter by and by.

Words and tune BY AND BY, Charles A. Tindley, c. 1905; altered and arranged, B. B. McKinney, 1937.

9
"Singing Is for Believers"

As we appraise the role of B. B. McKinney, three facets stand out. First, the music he wrote was in response to human need, whether in his own life (such as "Satisfied with Jesus") or in the life of another (Robert S. Jones in "Wherever He Leads I'll Go"). Second, he was person-centered, uncluttered with the details of administration. Third, he was a congregational song leader more than a choral director.

To illustrate these facets, let's listen to more of his friends who knew him.

As to his uncluttered life, Porter W. Routh told me that McKinney "was a country boy from Louisiana with a good dose of religion, coupled with a black music background featuring rhythm of heart, head, and feet."

Routh, a nephew of Leila Routh McKinney, continued, "He wasn't a theologian, just a man with a strong faith in God. A loving person, he liked to play with kids. When we moved to Nashville, our youngsters enjoyed going over to Uncle Mac's. He'd pick them up and rough-house with them. He wasn't stand-offish."

For more on his life-style, we turn to Clifford A. Holcomb, who came to the Church Music Department in Nashville as a staff member in early 1953. "McKinney was not a detail man," Holcomb wrote me. "He almost detested office work such as keeping files and dictating letters. Even when I came to Nashville, four months after his death, we continued to find letters, poems, manuscripts, and the like in files, desk drawers, and pockets of his suits with no evidence that the matters had ever been properly handled—and little indication as to whom the items belonged to."

As for writing music to meet human need, let's consider two examples. Both the words and the tune of "When the Morning Comes," reproduced at the front of this chapter, were written in 1907. The author and the composer was Charles A. Tindley, a distinguished black Methodist pastor in Philadelphia. McKinney did a slight alteration of the text and harmonization for use in *The Broadman Hymnal* in 1940.

One reason McKinney focused on this hymn was in response to a tragedy in the family of his oldest sister, Joanna McKinney Davis. Carolyn Davis McFarland, one of Joanna's daughters, told me the story in a telephone interview on August, 11, 1984:

> On Thanksgiving Day, 1931, my brother, Morgan, shot himself accidentally. He was a deputy sheriff in Minden, Louisiana and had just brought some prisoners in from the fields where they'd been working, as it started to rain.
>
> Morgan sat down at a long, low table to drink coffee. As he leaned back, his revolver fell on the floor, discharged, and sent a bullet through the bench and into his head, back of the ear. He died instantly.
>
> There were no phones then, so my Uncle Will came out to our place. He couldn't say anything, just walked the floor. Then he asked the menfolk to go out to the barn with him, where he told them. Then he added, "But I can't tell Sis." One of my brothers volunteered, so they came back inside.
>
> "Sit down, Mama, we've got something to tell you," he began. "Tell me quick—I know it's bad," she answered, for she never wanted anything kept back, good or bad. When Mama learned the tragic news, she said, "It's the Lord's will." She was a strong woman; we never saw her shed a tear, although she was in shock.
>
> But after that, we could hear Daddy crying in the night and Mother comforting him. Daddy kept saying he couldn't understand it, that if Morgan hadn't been sheriff, this wouldn't have happened.

Their sorrow focused McKinney's interest in "When the Morning Comes," which closes, "We will understand it better by and by." Carolyn remembers the comfort this song was to her parents and family.

Another good example of writing to meet human need is "Wherever He Leads I'll Go." Kathleen Jones, M.D., Southern Baptist missionary to Indonesia, wrote me on January 23, 1984:

> My father was Robert S. Jones from Murray, Kentucky. He was a missionary to Brazil for ten years, then from 1932-1943 was an assistant secretary in the Foreign Mission Board offices at Richmond. From there he went to the Annuity Board in Dallas, where he was director of investments until his retirement in 1957.
>
> He and B. B. had been friends for years. I don't recall the year he saw Dr. McKinney at Falls Creek, but it was probably 1930 or 1931 when we were living on Seminary Hill in Fort Worth.
>
> B. B., aware of my father's health problems, was talking with him one afternoon. He'd just received a letter from the Foreign Mission Board, saying this was the last salary check the one hundred missionaries home on furlough would receive.
>
> The future was very uncertain (both health-wise and financial). So B. B. asked Dad, "What will you do now?" He said he didn't know, but "Wherever God leads, I'll go."
>
> Dr. McKinney then went to his room, wrote the words and tune, and sang it that night. We have it in Indonesian and it has been translated into Portuguese. A music missionary in Brazil says it is a favorite there.

Dr. Jones had come home from Brazil in 1930 with a severe case of bronchial pneumonia. His health never allowed him to return, even when finances got better at the Foreign Mission Board.

William J. Reynolds tells a slightly different version in his book *Companion to Baptist Hymnal*. Reynolds says the McKinney-Jones conversation took place in Clanton, Alabama on January 15-17, 1936, during the Alabama Sunday School Convention. Reynolds says McKinney wrote the hymn while at this convention and sang it as a solo at the closing session.

My guess is the hymn had been crystallizing in McKinney's mind since 1931, that he had sung bits and pieces of it here and there, and by 1936 had finalized it on paper. For one thing, by 1936 Jones had already been in his new job in Richmond for four years. The cricitical years when his future was uncertain were 1930-31, the time Kathleen remembers him being at Falls Creek with McKinney.

Such details, however, are not all that important. What matters is that McKinney was a sensitive person who could reach out in his music to a denominational executive as well as a Louisiana farm woman. And in a period during 1926 as a seminary professor, dissatisfied with his spiritual maturity, he could sit at his desk at Southwestern Baptist Seminary and write "Satisfied with Jesus."

Last, some appraisals of his role as a congregational song leader by J. O. Strother of Bangs, Texas, who knew him for many years:

> We had a piano in our home and one of the joys each summer was to get the new Robert Coleman revival song book and learn the new McKinney songs.
>
> In my youth, I observed him direct the singing at some of our state conventions. He had a relaxed and informal way that just made people want to sing. He didn't look as if he were fighting bumblebees. He told us, "I announce the number, set the tempo, and get out of the way."

And from Angleton, Texas Jack Chastain wrote me:

> As a child, age 6 to 12, I remember B. B. McKinney leading the singing at Siloam Springs Baptist Encampment in Arkansas.
>
> He was truly blessed of God in getting music out of a congregation. He didn't wiggle a finger or act like he was conducting a trio. He made no apologies. He seemed to treat his congregation as a mass choir and expected everyone to sing.
>
> I'm thinking how he taught us to sing "Never Alone." After we'd sung the first verse, he said we sounded like a "sick or dying calf." Then, to illustrate, he sang the words "no-ooo never alone" in a slurring fashion. He then insisted that the "No!" be sung almost staccato.
>
> To this day, I hear song leaders who fail to understand what he

was saying when he arranged "Never Alone" on page 400 of *The Broadman Hymnal*.

From Taiwan, Southern Baptist missionaries Ruth and Art Robinson wrote that "We never rubbed shoulders with B. B., but his songs really rubbed off on us. Our Chinese choir at Trinity Baptist Church in Tainan sings 'Glorious Is Thy Name.' We have an old hand-me-down set of *The Broadman Hymnal* that we draw on for specials."

Of all the letters I received about the joy of McKinney-led congregational singing, one of the best came from a woman who now lives in a senior citizens center. She is Beatrice Murray Rice of Oklahoma City, and here's how she put it, in her own words:

Who could ever forget that giant song bird? He was Mr. Music, Mr. Falls Creek!

It must have been the early 1940s. We were from Irving, a small mission sponsored by Kellham Avenue Baptist Church. We stayed in Tent City.

"Glorious Is Thy Name" was the favorite that summer. Our singing lifted that tabernacle roof at least six inches every night.

One night after lights out, rain awakened Tent City. Our group had two tents—one for protecting our food and cooking utensils, and one to store our clothing. We slept on cots under the trees.

We all jumped up, put on shoes or whatever, rolled up our bedding, and ran to the tents. No sleep—wet clothes—crammed under those tents like sardines. But listen! Someone, somewhere on that mountain began singing: "Glor . . . ri . . . ous, Glo . . . ri . . . ous, Glo . . . ri . . . ous is Thy name, O Lord!"

Soon those mountains were alive in heavenly chorus as singers from every camp joined in. Heaven came down and glory filled our souls. "The mountains and the hills shall break forth before you into singing, and all the trees of the field shall clap their hands" (Isa. 55:12). "And the little hills rejoice on every side" (Ps. 65:12).

Remember one of the first things McKinney told Warren Angell at Oklahoma Baptist University—"You direct the choirs; I'll lead the congregation." Indeed, he considered every congregation a mass choir.

Can B. B. McKinney teach us something in our churches today? Oh, I don't mean how to sing "Never Alone." I mean his insistence that no choir or soloist, however trained, can take the place of congregational singing.

Donald Hustad, a music professor at The Southern Baptist Theological Seminary in Louisville, Kentucky and frequent organist for Billy Graham crusades, wrote something in the Winter 1982 issue of *Leadership* magazine that caught my eye. He said, "Somehow, about forty percent of churchgoers seem to have picked up the idea that 'singing in church is for singers.' The truth is that 'singing is for believers.' The relevant question is not, 'Do you have a voice?' but 'Do you have a song?'"

C. L. Minton of Snyder, Texas sounded this warning in a letter to the editor in the January 23, 1985 issue of *The Baptist Standard*. In it he said, "Southern Baptists are in danger of losing their tradition of a 'singing' faith' by letting special groups provide music instead of the congregation."

John P. Newport, a vice-president at Southwestern Baptist Theological Seminary in Fort Worth, Texas, addressed the same subject in the January 1984 issue of *Baptist History and Heritage*. He said that from their beginnings in America, Baptists identified with the common people. He said this popular approach, which continues today, is based in part on music, which appeals to the masses "and is adaptable and portable."

And Bruce Leafblad, in a July 13, 1984 *Baptist Press* feature, warned that in many churches today the singing of the congregation (the largest musical group in any church) is viewed as the least important. He traced part of the problem to the 1960s when musical groups began to be emphasized. "We started doing music for the people and not letting them do the music," he said. "We need the music restored to the people."

Leafblad, a music professor at Southwestern Baptist Seminary, criticized the spiritual depth of some music being written today. He lamented that "every Tom, Dick, and Harry is writing music, so-called, for the church today."

And Charles Willis quotes Jean Pilcher on the same theme in another *Baptist Press* feature dated July 27, 1984. Pilcher, minister of music at the

First Baptist Church in Little Rock, Arkansas, sees a long-standing trend toward worship as a spectator experience. She fears many churchgoers think of congregational singing as "something that happens before something else happens."

In the same *Baptist Press* feature, William J. Reynolds says he's heard Southern Baptists in many settings as they engaged in both "hearty singing and holy mumbling." Reynolds laments that at the same time we've seen a growth in graded choirs, "congregations have become listeners and watchers." He said he's not happy until "I have everybody singing." Reynolds writes out of long observation, for he was one of McKinney's successors as secretary of the Church Music Department and has directed the singing at numerous sessions of the Southern Baptist Convention, as well as the Baptist World Alliance.

And on the sidelines, B. B. McKinney would say, "Amen!"

For the closing lines of this biography, let's go back to the boyhood scenes of B. B. McKinney in Webster Parish, not far from Minden and Heflin, Louisiana. At one time during my research, I considered a trip down there, and still hope to go someday. His niece, Carolyn Davis McFarland of Route 1, Heflin, wrote me:

> I think your visit to Heflin would be a disappointment. There are pine trees for miles and miles—no signs of the McKinney homeplace. Heflin is a small "ghost" town with one store, a post office, two churches and an elementary school. Some dairy farming, but no field farming or open fields.
>
> All of the people who knew the McKinneys are passed away. Most of those left are in their 70s. We recently built a new church. . . . when the cornerstone was laid, it had books of B. B. McKinney and write-ups about him."

The landmarks may be gone. But the memories—and the songs—live on!

For Further Reading

I purposefully didn't clutter this book with footnotes, lest it read like a dissertation. Documentation is in the form of my own interview notes, clippings, correspondence, and tape recordings. All of this is deposited in the McKinney Collection at the Dargan Research Library, 127 Ninth Avenue, North, Nashville, Tennessee 37234.

Researchers will find little additional factual information in this collection. What they will find is my voluminous correspondence from persons all over the country. It was impossible to quote everyone in the book. Also included are many of the letters Mrs. McKinney received at his death in 1952. Dr. McKinney saved little of his own correspondence.

A number of persons, such as Winborn E. Davis, James L. Sullivan, William J. Reynolds, Albert McClellan, J. D. Grey, Clifford A. Holcomb, W. Hines Sims, Wesley Forbis, and James McKinney sent one or more summaries of their recollections.

I also deposited the notes I made when interviewing such persons as Mrs. McKinney, her sons Eugene and B. B., Jr., Carolyn Davis McFarland, Winborn E. Davis, Mrs. John W. Raley, Warren M. Angell, Porter W. Routh, and Henry C. McGill, Jr., M.D.

The Nashville collection also includes:

(1) A chapel message by William J. Reynolds at Southwestern Baptist Theological Seminary on September 20, 1979, "I. E. Reynolds, Church Music Crusader."

(2) A transcript of a significant conversation between T. L. Holcomb, W. Hines Sims, and William J. Reynolds, taped on September 20, 1965 at the Hermitage Hotel in Nashville.

(3) An unpublished paper by McKinney, about 1942, "Plans for Promoting Church Music."

(4) An interview of Mrs. McKinney by J. M. Gaskin when she helped dedicate a historical marker at Falls Creek on August 8, 1978.

(5) An unpublished paper by Mrs. McKinney, "Treasures," which details her childhood, among other things.

In my research, I was given hundreds of unidentified family photos and snapshots, apparently of McKinney grandchildren and other relatives. These are also in the Nashville collection.

A microfilm, "The Published Works of B. B. McKinney," compiled by Mrs.

McKinney, is also at Dargan Research Library. The original is at Oklahoma Baptist University. Each Southern Baptist seminary library also has a copy.

The B. B. McKinney Music Research Foundation was established at Oklahoma Baptist University in 1954. Here are the original bound copies of "The Published Works of B. B. McKinney." Also there are about seven hundred books once owned by McKinney, including a large collection of hymnals and gospel song books, some from the nineteenth century.

While on the O. B. U. campus in August of 1984, J. M. Gaskin and I found a "wire recording" made by Dr. and Mrs. McKinney at their Nashville home during Christmas of 1946. (Wire recordings—so named because the recording was made on a thin filament or wire—were the forerunners of tape recorders.) It was a recorded greeting, plus several solos, to a church in Dallas where he'd been in a revival the preceding year. The recording was in poor condition, so we transferred it onto a cassette tape. Just as we finished, the original "wire" broke and wound itself into an irretrievable jumble. The recording includes "Wayfaring Stranger." The quality is poor, but his personality comes through. I have since learned other copies exist of this recording.

The Norton Memorial Library at Louisiana College in Pineville has a limited collection. I did not go there, but Landrum Salley told me it includes interviews with some McKinney relatives. Chiefly, it consists of copies of manuscripts from the Nashville and O. B. U. collections.

The most succinct treatment of McKinney's life is an eleven-page biographical sketch in William J. Reynolds' book *The Songs of B. B. McKinney* (Nashville: Broadman Press, 1974). Actually, it's a McKinney hymnbook, for it includes 137 hymns written or arranged by him.

J. M. Gaskin's book *Sights and Sounds of Falls Creek* devotes some space to McKinney, the memorial chapel, and E. E. "Hot Dog" Lee (Oklahoma City: Baptist Messenger Press, 1980).

Insights into McKinney's friendship with Dr. and Mrs. John W. Raley and Warren M. Angell at Oklahoma Baptist University are treated in Mrs. Raley's book, *Angell!* (Norman, Oklahoma: Transcript Press, 1982).

Sixteen hymns either written or arranged by McKinney are in the 1975 *Baptist Hymnal*. The stories back of those hymns are told in *Companion to Baptist Hymnal* by William J. Reynolds (Nashville: Broadman Press, 1976).

Paul R. Powell wrote a master's thesis, "A Biographical and Bibliographical Study of B. B. McKinney," which is in the library of New Orleans Baptist Seminary. Powell adapted this thesis into a forty-eight-page booklet, *Wherever He Leads I'll Go* (New Orleans: Insight Press, 1974).

Other helpful books include:

The Sunday School Board: Ninety Years of Service by Walter B. Shurden (Nashville: Broadman Press, 1981).

Let Us Sing, by B. B. McKinney and Allen W. Graves (Nashville: Broadman Press, 1981).

Makers of Music by Novella Preston Jordan (Nashville: Broadman Press, 1982).

Know Your Hymns, by Edmond D. Keith and Gaye L. McGlothlen (Nashville: Convention Press, 1962).

Hymns of Our Faith, by William J. Reynolds (Nashville: Broadman Press, 1964).

Of the magazine articles dealing with McKinney, here are five of the best:

"Mrs. B. B. McKinney" by Dorothy Baskin and Leonard Hill, September 1977 issue of *Mature Living*.

"We Sing His Songs" by William J. Reynolds, April 1986 issue of *Church Administration*.

"The Singing Home of B. B. McKinney" by Beth Prim, August 1948 issue of *Home Life*.

"Over Jordan" by Hines Sims and Novella D. Preston, December 1952 issue of *The Church Musician*.

"Monument to B. B. McKinney" by Joan Harvison, August 1966 issue of *The Church Musician*.

Three unpublished dissertations deserve reading:

"Musical Evangelism of the Southern Baptist Home Mission Board (1910-1928)" by William L. Haas, Jr., Library, New Orleans Baptist Theological Seminary.

"The Contribution of Isham E. Reynolds to Church Music in the Southern Baptist Convention Between 1915-1945" by Tommy R. Spigener, Library, Southwestern Baptist Theological Seminary.

"The Southern Baptist Sunday School Board's Program of Church Music" by Floyd H. Patterson, Library, George Peabody College for Teachers, Nashville.

And finally, Vol. 2, p. 842, *The Encyclopedia of Southern Baptists* includes "McKinney, Baylus Benjamin" by Josephine Pile (Nashville: Broadman Press, 1958).